SpringerBriefs in Economics

For further volumes:
http://www.springer.com/series/8876

Alexander Krauss

External Influences and the Educational Landscape

Analysis of Political, Economic, Geographic, Health and Demographic Factors in Ghana

Springer

Dr. Alexander Krauss
The World Bank Group
Washington, DC
USA

ISSN 2191-5504 ISSN 2191-5512 (electronic)
ISBN 978-1-4614-4935-5 ISBN 978-1-4614-4936-2 (eBook)
DOI 10.1007/978-1-4614-4936-2
Springer New York Heidelberg Dordrecht London

Library of Congress Control Number: 2012945100

Printed on acid-free paper

Springer is part of Springer Science+Business Media (www.springer.com)

Abstract

While the analysis is not the first to investigate empirically the effects of different individual or household factors on school access and completion of Ghanaians, it extends previous work by simultaneously incorporating individual, household, community, regional and national characteristics and also illustrates the latest evidence by applying international data sources and unusually detailed household survey data for a sub-Saharan country. Its focus is threefold: (1) gaining a richer understanding of which external influences hinder educational access and attainment in Ghana, (2) how to better tackle these challenges and (3) analysing how educational development affects the country's overall development. An interview with the Minister of Education helps guide the policy orientation of the analysis by identifying several critical challenges and areas of needed policy attention. Findings from the data analysis indicate that the geographic divide between the North and South, increased economic growth, demographic pressure and a number of individual, household and community factors especially children's nutritional and labour status are the most important challenges in increasing levels of education among Ghanaians in years to come. Finally, the analysis pilots a new and comprehensive results- and capacity-focused policy matrix to help the Government of Ghana realign policy priorities and reform existing programmes. To this end, respective policy levers on the demand- and supply-side are discussed, with particular reference to external and demand-side interventions which have not received the necessary attention at the policy-level to improve educational opportunities and outcomes at all levels.

Acknowledgment

I am grateful to the Ghanaian Statistical Service and the World Bank for access and permission to a number of household survey data sets, and thankful for comments from my three reviewers Prof. Dr. Helmut Asche (University of Leipzig, Faculty of History, Arts and Oriental Studies), Prof. Lant Pritchett (Harvard University, Kennedy School of Government) and Dr. Ishac Diwan (Harvard University, Kennedy School of Government), as well as from Josie Stewart (Africa Governance Initiative), Corinna Peters (GIZ), Michele Savini (Government of Ghana), Kazimir Menzel (University of Heidelberg) and Sarah Brierley (World Bank). The author presented the key findings and defended the work in January 2012 at the University of Leipzig where it was submitted as part of his doctoral requirements. He can be contacted at akrauss@worldbank.org or alexander_krauss@hotmail.de.

Contents

Chapter 1
Introduction

Low levels of education remain one of Ghana's most fundamental challenges to increased human and economic welfare. While the extent of educational coverage among different groups in Ghanaian society at a given period of time depends on a number of variables, education development in Ghana overall seems to be strongly driven by various external factors (defined here as non-education specific factors at the personal, family, community, regional and national level). The basic argument, education development cannot be seen without viewing geography, macroeconomic trends, demographic patterns and the overall external environment, is explored here. The analysis investigates issues such as: what role does urbanisation play in education service delivery, how does economic growth impact government spending on education, to which extent does population growth put pressure on new enrolments, whether geographic remoteness continues to keep children out of school, if malnourished or anaemic children are more likely to start late and miss school, when changes in the political environment matter for education development, why many children assist in family farming activities instead of attending school, among others. The social and policy importance of these questions was also underlined during an interview for this analysis with the Minister of Education, Hon. Alex Tettey-Enyo, confirming the "need to look at the constraining factors that impede the mobilisation or recruitment of the [last] 10 % into the school system". Though, often economists and at times policy-makers, who indeed break out of supply-side thinking, focus their attention on how household income is associated with access to education and how access affects household income. Analyses of the causes of inequitable schooling that do attempt to broaden their scope generally will only include gender and rural/urban dimensions. Other factors, however, such as the geographic marginalisation of the North, population growth, macroeconomic conditions as well as background characteristics such as children's labour and nutritional status can affect educational opportunities and outcomes more strongly within the Ghanaian context, as the present study shows.

As children are the economy's future human resources and are thus at the forefront of the country's future development, completion of at least basic education for all children in Ghana is a fundamental prerequisite for sustainable national development. Nonetheless, data calculations of the 2008/2009 Ghana Demographic and Health Survey indicate that about one in every four youth 17–19 years of age

A. Krauss, *External Influences and the Educational Landscape*,
SpringerBriefs in Economics, DOI: 10.1007/978-1-4614-4936-2_1,

(24.6 %) have not finished primary schooling and over half of all youth of this age (56.5 %) have not completed the basic education cycle, in spite of policies making these levels 'free, compulsory and universal'. The challenge is even more serious, as about one in every six children 6–14 years old (15.6 %) did not even attend school in the academic year 2008/2009. Most forms of educational deprivation also increase by each higher class, so that the completion of upper secondary and especially higher education is exclusively reserved for a very small share of privileged Ghanaians. Given this context, the analysis examines access to and completion of different levels of education (generally, no schooling, primary, lower and upper secondary and higher education). Taking a systemic approach, it seeks to address the following core questions:

- How and to what extent do political, economic, geographic, health and demographic factors affect educational access and attainment in Ghana?
- How and to what extent does educational attainment influence political, economic, health and demographic factors in Ghana?
- In response to the key findings, what combinations of policies and programmes are likely to lead to the greatest access and attainment in Ghana especially for educationally deprived groups in years to come?

When relevant and data is available, trends are examined over the past few decades, especially the 1990s and 2000s. Answers to these questions are critical for planners and policy-makers in Ghana. In particular, identifying which external constraints and enabling factors are most important and which policies are therefore best in promoting the educational status of Ghanaians is an underlying issue guiding this analysis.

The scope, nature, evolution and implications of the interrelationships between education and outside influences (influences outside of the classroom) are examined. By analysing trends at the macro and micro level and by applying an inter-sectoral approach, a deeper understanding of the combination of contextual factors interacting throughout different stages of access to and transition through education is possible. This is not to say that external- and demand-side interventions are to be the central focus of education policy. Especially in upper secondary schooling and beyond, widening the supply of education services will continue to exercise leverage and impact, but overall greater external- and demand-side interventions are needed to improve access to, participation in and completion of education at all levels. At the same time, the Minister of Education affirmed during the interview that the government "wants to look more into the demand side". After the data analysis, the study identifies demand- and supply-side solutions and outlines these possibilities.

The analysis explores the extent to which public education policy that is largely supply-orientated has limited reach, effectiveness and sustainability in the process of improving educational access and completion. It argues that to provide equitable opportunities in basic education for all Ghanaians, the education sector and a wider range of policy instruments cannot be separated from the overall external environment within which the sector operates and which presents constraints and opportunities that face the sector. As a country with for example a high annual population growth (slightly over 2 % based on 2010 UN population data) and a relatively high foreign debt burden (averaging 8 % during 2000–2008 based on World Development data), Ghana's overall development is confronted with multiple challenges. Simultaneously however, the country also has several opportunities, with historically the highest GDP growth attained over the period 2000–2008 at 5.3 % annually (World Development data) and with the country's transition to middle-income status as of November 2010 (Ghana Statistical Service 2010).

Problem Statement, Significance and Strategic Orientation

While much research exists on what happens inside the classroom in affecting the schooling experience of children and youth, much less exists on what happens outside the classroom in influencing initial entry to, progression through or completion of different educational cycles. In Ghana, as internationally, household survey analysis on factors outside the classroom tends to largely focus on the linkage between two variables: how household income levels relate to educational opportunities and vice versa, with little attention to a wide-range of external factors (a few examples are: Nsowah-Nuamah et al. 2010; Teal 2001; Jolliffe 2002; Rolleston and Oketch 2007; Buchmann et al. 2001, p. 94). A review of the prevailing literature—as shown throughout the analysis—confirms that no comprehensive and differential diagnosis on Ghana's education development has been conducted incorporating the role of both micro- and macro-economic variables with the broad spectrum of non-economic factors such as political, geographic, health and demographic variables. This is, however, not the first analysis to explore the interactions between schooling and different individual- or household-level influences within Ghana, but it goes beyond this scope to include individual, family, community, regional and national factors at once, using the most recent data available. The motivation for this analysis is, in addition, born out of the shortcomings of the government's annually produced Education Sector Performance Reports (e.g. Ministry of Education 2010) and a recently published World Bank (2011) report, which attempt to provide a comprehensive diagnosis of the education sector's performance in Ghana despite the fact that their orientation is principally on sector-specific issues. It also partly arises out of the current academic literature's strong attention on a limited number of variables influencing schooling opportunities, particularly school-level supply factors and household income but also gender and rural/urban dimensions. By turning the central focus to the wide-range of external factors at both the macro and micro levels, the analysis here attempts to fill this research gap and argues that outside influences can determine the performance of the sector more so than school-specific factors and therefore need to be much better reflected in policy formulation and programmes.

It is argued here that a central challenge facing education decision-makers in Ghana is to determine how to increase the efficiency and impact of existing and additional resources to improve levels of education, as the analysis identifies large public resource inefficiencies. Through a deepened and broadened understanding of the constraining and driving factors of education development, the primary objective of the analysis is therefore to help inform policy-makers and administrators on possible paths through which this challenge can be tackled, which will largely depend on identifying means to increase household demand for schooling and to better target existing programmes.

Within the framework of Ghana's 'Growth and Poverty Reduction Strategy' outlined in 2006, increasing human resources and the educational qualifications of the labour force is an area recognised as the focal point of strategy and the centre of domestic priorities for national development (NDPC 2005). Establishing which underlying factors pull and push changes in education indicators, implications at the policy level are drawn that may help to contribute to the government's overarching development strategy.

Research Methodology and Data

The analysis represents the culmination of 20 months of research carried out in Ghana between 2009 and 2011, with primary data analysis (interviews, policy dialogue and various fieldwork trips) conducted together with secondary data analysis (mostly employing household survey data and aggregate national data) to be able to better inform policy and practice.[1] For the purpose of this analysis an in-depth, semi-structured interview was conducted with the Minister of Education, Hon. Alex Tettey-Enyo, on 19 October 2010, which allows for a nuanced interpretation of the drivers and inhibitors of sectoral change at the policy formulation and implementation level. It is important to emphasise that the views expressed reflect the Minister's subjective standpoint and not necessary those of the Government of Ghana. His insight is a vital component of this analysis in order to assess the extent to which the sectoral needs and policy direction from the Minister's viewpoint coincide with the sectoral challenges established through the data analysis conducted here. A number of the Minister's views are discussed throughout sections of the analysis (a transcript of the full interview can be provided by contacting the author). To widen the spectrum and to deepen understanding of inter-locking factors, the study conducts a desk review of existing (mainly national but also international) literature published by development institutions, academics, civil society organisations and the government.

The study begins by exploring how various political and macroeconomic variables and mechanisms, which are not captured in household survey data but

[1] The author participated in direct policy dialogue on frequent occasions within the Ministry of Education in Ghana in collaboration with the World Bank from mid 2009 to early 2011.

rather in aggregate national data, correlate with and influence the education sector. For the chapters covering geography, health, microeconomics and demographics, the study seeks, largely by means of household data analysis, a better understanding of which multiple non-education specific factors influence educational access and attainment strongest, the forms of these relationships and potential determinants, and (when relevant) analyses these patterns and trends over the past few decades. Descriptive data analysis is often used as it can be at least as informative and useful for policy as regression analysis, which is also conducted when data allows and applicable. As part of the qualitative data collection for this analysis, 15 students from two schools (one primary and one upper secondary school) in the capital Accra were randomly selected and interviewed after school on the 23rd and 24th of September 2010 using semi-structured questions and methods (Van Evera 1997). The primary school provides services for poorer children while the upper secondary school for wealthier youth based on the author's observation. While it represents a very small sample of urban students—with 51 % of Ghanaians living within urban areas in 2009 (UN population data)—this qualitative field research is only intended to offer additional micro-level insight and detailed explanations that at times help to complement central findings from the household data analysis. Names have been omitted to preserve confidentiality. Indication of field research throughout respective sections of the analysis, unless otherwise indicated, refers to this data collection, or to policy dialogue if specified as such. These different research methods have been selected because combining such research approaches is possibly the most effective way to inform policy on the relative effects of external factors, whether at the individual, household, community or national level, on educational development, and vice versa. Final results are to be presented to senior officials and data technocrats within the Ministry of Education in Ghana.

Household survey data and other data sources. Household surveys allow for the monitoring and evaluating of policies over time. They also provide data on sectoral deficiencies and inter-connected relationships and as such offer a basis for evidence-based, informed decision-making. During the interview the Minister of Education affirmed that "you [the government] need a lot of data to be able to plan development—on all fronts". In this sense, the Ghana Demographic and Health Survey (GDHS) and the Ghana Living Standards Survey (GLSS) are vital for the planning of Ghanaian development, and are widely used and recognised as the most comprehensive and reliable sources of household data in the country among the latest data, as the literature review in this analysis also confirms. This analysis employs nationally representative household-level data based on the latest rounds of these two surveys, both of which are carried out by the Government of Ghana and used as one of the principal means to inform policy by the government itself and among others by multilateral development institutions. GDHS, which is the latest household survey data available in the country at the point that this analysis was finalised, covers 11,778 households for the 2008/2009 survey and, when trends over time are explored, the 1993/1994 survey is used, covering 5,822 households. The sample design involves selecting clusters from the 2000 Ghana Population and Housing Census using a systematic selection employing the 'probability proportional to size' method (for more information on the sample design and questionnaires see: GDHS 2009). In addition, data from GLSS, covering 8,687 households for the 2005/2006 survey and 4,552 households for the 1991/1992 survey, are also applied especially when specific economic indicators are analysed such as child labour, household income and school expenditure, given that GDHS does not capture these variables. Like GDHS, Ghana Living Standards Surveys are stratified by location and are clustered as census enumeration areas by also applying the 'probability proportional to size' method (for more information see: GLSS 2008). These national, cross-sectional surveys cover all ten regions of the country and collect information on between 20,000 and 47,000 household members. While these surveys have limitations on drawing policy implications from the findings at the district level, it is possible to derive conclusions and discuss policy options on a regional and national scale. Data employed for international comparisons and for the chapters covering political and macroeconomic factors are largely derived from the World Development Indicators database (2011) which reflects the most recent, precise and comprehensive international development data available and includes data on indicators compiled from officially-recognised international sources like UNESCO, OECD and WHO.

Government data and its limitations. Much of the analysis is based on household data given that field research here indicates that administrative data on education in Ghana, which are derived from the Education Management Information System (EMIS), have a number of limitations. First, information on education cannot be consistently compared to background characteristics at the individual, household and community level such as health conditions or household makeup. Second, EMIS data is adjusted for non-reporting schools that receive district averages, which is unlikely given that non-reporting schools are likely to be poorer performers. Third, there is the likelihood that some school officials report higher enrolment rates than actual values as the amount of government subsidies received, such as through the capitation grant which is per capita based, is higher for schools with higher reported enrolment rates. Fourth, government data does not capture the large numbers of children who drop out or never enrol at all. Fifth, the government collects data on school enrolment (not attendance) while it is possible that some children enrol into school formally but do not actually attend. Finally, most enrolment indicators using EMIS data are based on school-age population growth projections estimated at 2.7 % yearly since the 2000 census but much anecdotal evidence suggests this estimate is high. All limitations combined, the use of government data presents challenges for education policy planning and is to be interpreted with caution. This is where household surveys provide a complementary or alternative data source to administrative data (for a comprehensive analysis of the education sector using government data see: World Bank 2011). Administrative data made available by the Ministry of Education are at times nonetheless used, when applicable, in particular for comparative purposes.

The scope of the analysis. One of the main indicators used for the descriptive and regression data analysis is the number of years of schooling completed (educational attainment), which can indicate indirectly what amount of educational resources—physical, financial and human—has been allocated to the education sector, and is possibly the most comprehensive way to measure the state of education development in a given country by using only one indicator. From a cross-country educational perspective, the international community has focused on the second Millennium Development Goal which aims to "ensure that, by 2015, children everywhere, boys and girls alike, will be able to complete a full course of primary schooling" (World Bank 2009, p. 132). Completion rates are also commonly applied as a quality indicator in the literature (see e.g. World Bank 2010b). They capture quality by for example being the main determinant of literacy, as shown later by regression analysis. Descriptive GDHS data for 2008/2009 indicate that 98.3 % of 15–19 year old males without any schooling cannot read at all (neither part nor a whole sentence administered in the survey) while the share falls to 44.9 % for those with primary schooling and finally to 7.1 % for those with secondary schooling, with very similar shares for females. Other quality issues, despite their importance, are simply beyond the scope of this already extensive study that aims to comprehensively explore the complex dynamics of educational access, equity and attainment in the country. Apart from what can be achieved in a single study, a more narrowed research focus furthermore allows for a more detailed analysis. A study of the interactions between learning outcomes and a wide-range of outside influences—many of which (in contrast) can only indirectly influence the former—would be tied to even greater complexities but likely yield similar policy implications (to scale up external- and demand-side interventions), while the present study could nonetheless help to provide a foundation for such an analysis. With about 882,000 children of primary school-age and well over one million of basic school-age still outside of the school system based on 2008 World Bank Ed Stats data, there are more than enough children to justify a focused study on the causes of their educational exclusion. And continued analysis on out-of-school children and how to attract them into the system will likely remain an urgent need in Ghana for years to come. The resource allocations related to many of the current programmes, subsidies and safety nets aimed at increasing access and attainment are also large enough to warrant a study assessing ways to improve some of these interventions—the content of Chap. 8.

Besides completion rates, another central indicator used for the data analysis are school attendance rates. Finally, while the analysis also looks at the preschool and adult population, it by and large focuses on children aged 6–14 and youth aged 15–19 given their greater policy relevance.

Conceptual Framework

A conceptual framework outlined in Fig. 1.1 helps to guide the empirical analysis. It illustrates a wide-range of external factors to make influences and differences more detectable which would not be possible if the scope would be reduced to only analyse a few specific variables. It indicates that levels of education among

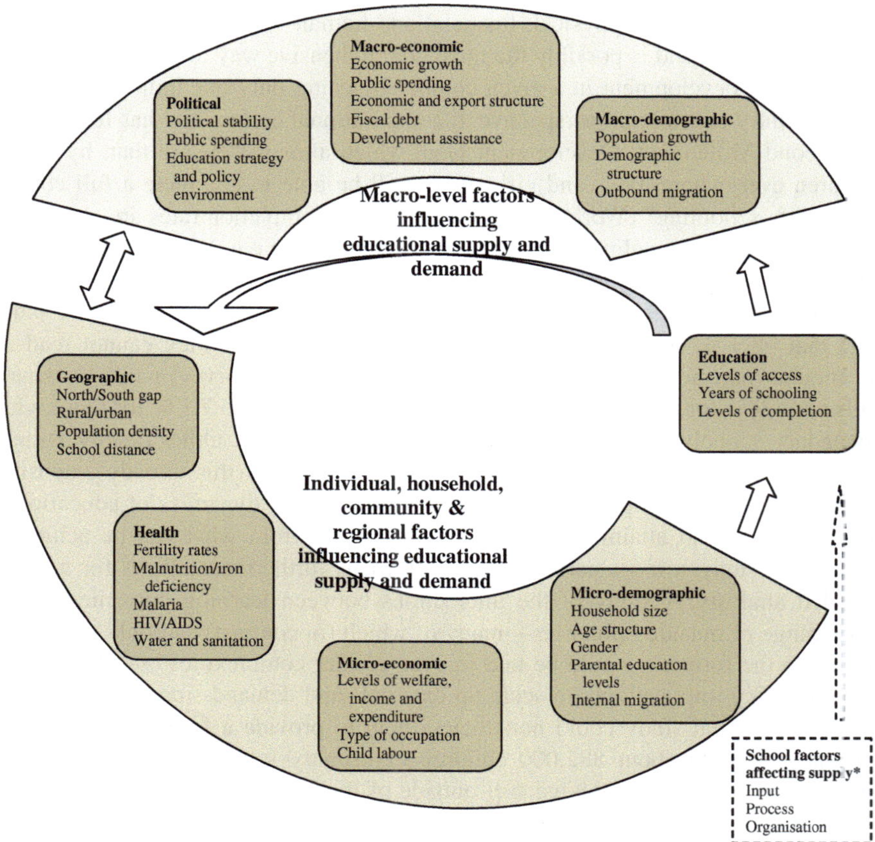

Fig. 1.1 Conceptual framework of factors helping to shape educational access and attainment in Ghana
Source Author's illustration based on the content of this analysis.
Note For simplification purposes, geographic factors are defined broadly throughout the analysis to incorporate both physical geography (covering the natural environment such as ecology) and human geography (covering cultural or built geography such as population density). *Research efforts in this analysis have limited focus on school-specific factors

different groups of Ghanaians are shaped by a number of interlocking factors at different levels, with relationships generally going in both directions. Overarching political, economic and demographic variables at the macro-level can promote or constrain the resources available for and demand of education at the individual, family, community and regional level, which in turn influence the underlying factors pulling and pushing individuals' educational and skills status. The decision to not complete basic schooling, drop out or not even enrol is rarely the consequence of one single risk factor or event, but rather a chain of events and factors, ranging from demographic growth (contributing to overcrowded classrooms) and geographic remoteness (distance to school) to malnutrition/stunting (giving way to late enrolment) and labour involvement (affecting school interruptions). That interactions go in both directions often implies that factors at the micro and macro levels affect the schooling opportunities available for children and youth early in life while the level of education they are able to acquire affects in turn a number of factors at these different levels later in life.

The rest of this study, after explaining the research interest, methodology and data sources here in the introduction, is organised as follows. Part I examines the constraints and opportunities posed by the political (Chap. 2) and macroeconomic (Chap. 3) environment in shaping the country's educational development and how its development in turn can influence this overall environment. Taking the constraining and enabling environment at the political and macroeconomic level into account, Part II then evaluates the interactions of various individual, household, community and regional characteristics (also some national factors) with educational development from four perspectives: geography (Chap. 4), health (Chap. 5), microeconomics (Chap. 6) and micro- and macro-demographics (Chap. 7). Building on the key challenges in achieving greater access and attainment at different levels of education identified in the preceding chapters, Chap. 8 assesses and develops a number of policy responses and packages that the government might consider. Chapter 9 sums up the general conclusions of the study, outlines lessons learned and coping strategies and identifies opportunities and emerging challenges.

Part I
The Political and Macroeconomic Environment for Education Development

Ghana has been widely recognised—within West Africa but also in Africa as a whole—as a regional success story. Contributing to this picture are: five successive peaceful elections, stable democratic institutions and good governance since 1992; solid macroeconomic management since 1983; and, among others, strong progress on the poverty reduction front, with 51.7 % of the population living below the national poverty line in 1992 reducing to 28.5 % by 2006 based on GLSS data. This strong performance has been influenced by and contributed to increased educational attainment, as the average years of schooling for the population aged 15 and above rose from 5.9 years in 1990 to 8 years in 2010 based on EdStats data.

The political and macroeconomic environment, its constraints and its conditions set the context within which the development of the education system can either be fostered or hindered. Within this context, however, scaling up educational opportunities and outcomes can also help to support the country's development by, for example, fostering political participation, helping to increase economic productivity and growth, and promoting poverty reduction and other key development objectives. In the two chapters that follow, the scope of both of these reinforcing dynamics are analysed.

Chapter 2
Political Environment: Stability, Public Spending and Policy

Access to and attainment of different levels of education depends on many interlocking factors coming together. Some of these are political. This chapter assesses the extent to which political stability influences educational opportunities and outcomes for Ghanaians through its effects on economic growth, public resource spending and education policy. It also explores, although to a lesser extent, how education can promote the consolidation of democratic institutions in Ghana.

Over the past three decades Ghana has been an exception in the West African coup d'état and civil war belt. Since Ghana gained independence in 1957, it has been one of the centrifugal forces of political transition on the continent. Especially over the last two decades, Ghana can be considered as one of the most politically stable countries both within West and sub-Saharan Africa. However, every country in West Africa has either gone through civil war over the past five to six decades or at the very least has not been able to maintain being (completely) politically stable (Boafo-Arthur 2008). Constantly relapsing coups and countercoups in West Africa have had catastrophic effects on the development processes of individual countries. A certain degree of political stability over time appears, however, to be a fundamental prerequisite for effective tax collection, public investments and national development—one may think of Liberia or Somalia. Large-scale conflict can therefore be seen as development in reverse. Many hospitals and school buildings, for instance, were completely destroyed due to armed conflicts in these countries. The fact that full-scale civil war never broke out in Ghana since independence has ensured not only more stable access to physical infrastructure like health facilities and schools but also ensured a more constant flow of financial resources as well as human resources such as doctors and teachers. In nearby conflict-prone countries, education sectors have in many cases regressed worse than levels decades ago. Sierra Leone, Nigeria and Liberia are a few examples (e.g. World Bank 2003).

Neighbouring Cote d'Ivoire, which has a similar ethnic composition and agro-ecological conditions (World Bank 2010d), is an example of a country considered stable like Ghana until 2002 when it became divided into a government-led South and a rebel-controlled North. This may offer some evidence of Ghana's vulnerability and how a country's development can at times hinge on political stability.

Simultaneously, however, democratic governance, a vibrant media, checks and balances, an active civil society—these are all terms commonly used to describe

A. Krauss, *External Influences and the Educational Landscape*,
SpringerBriefs in Economics, DOI: 10.1007/978-1-4614-4936-2_2,

Ghana's political development, as field research indicates. Ghana is classified as 'free' among only a few African countries by Freedom House (2010), implying that citizens in Ghana perceive that they are able to fully exercise their democratic freedoms.

Political (in-)stability affects (in-)stability in education expenditure and inputs. Ghana has not always been politically stable and experienced phases of severe political turbulence between the late 1960s and early 1980s. Only Nigeria had more successful military interventions (coup d'états) than Ghana within the West African region since 1960 (Boafo-Arthur 2008). As the first nation in sub-Saharan Africa free from colonial power, Kwame Nkrumah's new administration adopted an ambitious policy supporting the goal to reach 100 % literacy among the adult population (Glewwe and Ilias 1996). Over 50 years later, less than two-thirds of the adult population (62 %) were able to read and write in 2008, although multiple factors contribute to these low literacy levels relative to other middle income countries. Leading the Government of Ghana mostly with one-party politics, Nkrumah was overthrown in 1966 by military and police forces. Successive governments were also taken over by the military in 1972 and again in 1980, and eight additional coups took place, either attempted or palace coups, between 1966 and 1982 (Nketiah-Amponsah 2009). Figure 2.1 shows that the post-independence period until 1982 has been marked by constant and stark political instability (years of changes between civil governments and military regimes) that helped lead to fluctuations in GDP growth and in primary enrolment numbers, as government expenditure declined from 23.5 % of GDP in 1968 to only 7.3 % in 1983. As a result of the government's fiscal space slimming down, public spending on education reduced by 20 % over the period 1975–1980 and even by 17 % annually between 1980 and 1983 based on World Development data.

During this period of political and economic turbulence, primary enrolment figures increased by less than 200,000 children over two decades from around 1.1 million children (in 1966) to about 1.3 million (in 1985) in spite of rapid growth among the primary-age population and very large shares of out-of-school children, although enrolment rates over all these years are not available (Fig. 2.1). In fact, the number of children attending primary school reduced from about 1.5 million pupils in 1981 to about 1.3 million in 1985, with the rural poor likely accounting for the majority of these over 200,000 children pushed out of the system. That is, primary enrolment figures dropped by 13.7 % during this 4-year period. Exacerbating the economic downturn—and at the same time resulting from it—thousands of Ghanaian teachers migrated to Nigeria, where at the time oil discoveries had been made and the government was able to offer more attractive salary incentives for foreign teachers (Akyeampong et al. 2007). These uncertain times also led to diminished school supplies and reduced learning quality within schools in Ghana (Glewwe and Jacoby 1994).

In the post-1982 period, especially having returned from authoritarian rule to a multiparty democracy in 1992, GDP growth stabilised and government expenditure increased from 12.5 % of GDP in 1990 to about 30 % by 2010, giving way to a nearly 3-fold increase in public spending. As a result of these favourable political conditions, particularly since 1992, governments have been much more

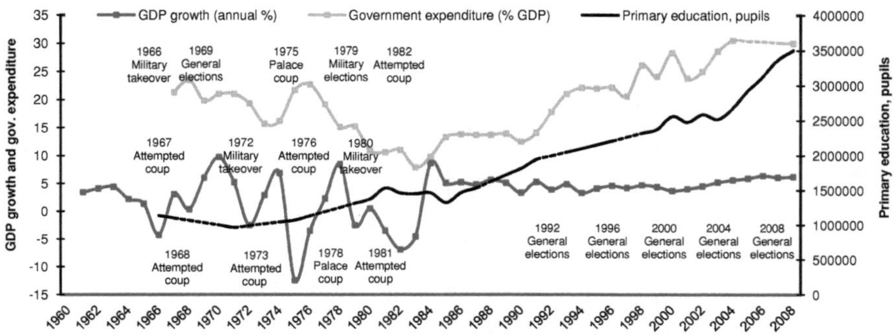

Fig. 2.1 Political status and GDP growth, public expenditure and primary enrolments in Ghana, 1960–2008.
Source Author's illustration based on data from World Development Indicators; data on political change based largely on Nketiah-Amponsah 2009.
Note The line is *dotted* when no data is available for a given year

successful in widening access to primary education so that 3.5 million children were enrolled in primary school by 2008 when, according to World Development data, net enrolment in primary reached 73.9 %, up from 52.4 % in 1990. In sum, the data provides evidence that political stability is strongly correlated with increased government spending and improved school enrolment in Ghana.

At independence, when Nkrumah's Convention People's Party began to initiate a reversal of the policy neglect of Northern Ghana with particular attention given to education, there was only one secondary school in the North of the country, located in Tamale (World Bank 2010d). When Nkrumah's Government collapsed through a coup d'état, so did his socialist agenda with ambitious education and economic objectives. It is worth noting that the populist Governments in Ghana, whether authoritarian or democratic, appear to have been the most proactive in promoting educational reforms aimed at widening opportunities and better serving the educational needs of the poor—the Governments of Nkrumah, the National Redemption Council, and Rawlings are examples (Little 2010).

Education development has been largely dependent on political stability since Rawlings' administration. With Rawlings' Government in the early 1980s came a return to relative stability, as structural reforms benefited the economy, stable GDP growth was recorded once again and public spending on education as a share of total government expenditure had slightly risen. President Rawlings, who ruled for about two decades until 2000, had a relatively strong support base within the poorest regions (especially in the North) which were recipients for the first time of targeted developmental programmes in education and health, water and road access and rural electrification (Haynes 1993). Rawlings' administration may provide some evidence that pro-poor investments in education and a stable increase in primary enrolments are at times tied to political stability.

Public spending on education fluctuates among different political regimes. Table 2.1 explores the question: to what extent do variations exist in shares of

Table 2.1 Public spending on education by political administration since independence

	Convention People's Party (Nkrumah)	National Liberation Council (Military Regime)	Busia Government (Progress Party)	National Redemption Council, Supreme Military Council	Supreme Military Council	Armed Forces Revolutionary Council (Rawlings)	Limann Government (People's National Party)	Provisional National Defence Council (Rawlings)	NDC (Rawlings)	NPP (Kufuor)	NDC (Mills)
Years in power	57′–66′	66′–69′	69′–72′	72′–78′	78′–79′	79′–79′	79′–81′	81′–93′	93′–01′	01′–09′	09′–
Years w/available data	–	–	*71′*	*75′*	–	–	*80–81′*	*85–90′*	*95–99′*	*05′*	*09′*
Average public spending on education, % of GDP	–	–	4.2	4.9	–	–	3.6	2.9	4.4	5.4	10
Public spending on education, % of gov. exp.	–	–	19.6	19.6	–	–	17.1	21.6	21.4	–	31

Source Author's calculations based on data from Africa Development Indicators government expenditure on education among different political administrations since independence? It indicates, although data is limited across all years, that public spending on education, both as a share of government expenditure or GDP, has overall been on the rise, in particular over the late 2000s. This implies that average education expenditure has generally been higher under democratic administrations. This could be partly explained by the fact that the advent of free and fair elections in 1992 (when President Rawlings stood for elections and won), with especially the 2000 and 2008 elections that helped to consolidate Ghana's democracy, made presidents more responsive and accountable to their constituents' needs for public investments.

Ghana's public resource envelope is large relative to other sub-Saharan economies. Through tax collection, which depends on a certain degree of state capacity and stability, the public sector spends resources aimed at achieving a number of national objectives. The public resource pool can be viewed as the government's principal policy tool to finance development programmes. Relative to other sub-Saharan economies, Ghana's government revenue as a share of GDP (excluding grants) is higher than most. In 2007, the latest year with comparative data, government revenue accounted for 25.7 % of GDP in Ghana, which was higher than neighbouring Cote d'Ivoire (19.2 %), Togo (17.0 %) and Burkina Faso (13.0 %) and only slightly below the world average (26.7 %).

The provision of educational services is partly dependent on the amount of public revenue at the government's disposal and by decisions about the share of public spending on education relative to other sectors competing for government funds. Determining the share and total of expenditure for each sector needed for development targets is central to effective policy-making. At the same time, using public spending as the sole measurement to assess how dedicated a government is to education can be imperfect since for example the degree of private sector involvement in education provision—although generally a small share—differs between countries. In Ghana, about four in every five students attended a government school at the basic level in 2009/2010, accounting for 80.5 % of pre-schoolers, 81.4 % of primary students and 82.6 % of lower secondary students (89.2 % and 86 % in upper secondary and tertiary, respectively) while the remaining attend private schools based on administrative EMIS data. Like in most developing countries, the government in Ghana is therefore the principal service deliverer of schooling.

Education is the largest (but most vulnerable) public good in Ghana. The degree of public spending on education is nonetheless generally a good measure of the priority that the government gives education compared to other sectors. By receiving the largest share of government spending, education appears to be the central priority of the government over the past decades (Fig. 2.2). At the same time, fluctuations in education expenditure have been very large over the years: even when overall government funds nearly doubled from 13.7 to 25 % of GDP during the period 1987–2002, the share of government resources committed to education nearly halved over this period from 26.5 to 14 % (ibid.). It is important to note that the overall fluctuations in education spending imply that uncertainties exist in the availability of resources to finance teacher salaries, school infrastructure and materials, and support incentive schemes to improve outcomes. However, even in the presence

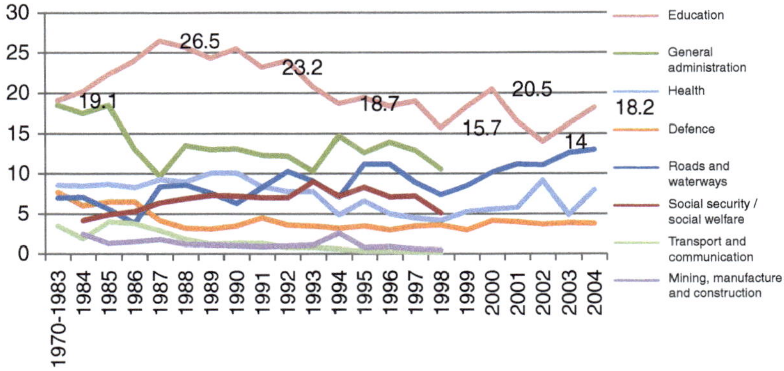

Fig. 2.2 Trends and structure of public expenditure (% of total) by sector, 1970–2004.
Source Illustration based on data from Nketiah-Amponsah (2009) using data compiled from the Ghana Statistical Service; Africa Development Indicators; and different budget statements.
Note The share for 1970–1983 reflects the average over these years

of this decline in education expenditure due to shifting sectoral priorities, the influence of political stability over this period on economic growth and government expenditure appears to have led to enrolment growth, as shown above in Fig. 2.1.

By 2010, the Government of Ghana was allocating about one-third of public expenditure to education including about 40 % of the total civil service to the sector (World Bank 2011). While stable and sufficient flows of education resources are a precondition, they will not be enough to guarantee advancements in attaining the education MDG and in promoting skills development, for which innovative ways to raise demand, widen opportunities and maximise resource efficiency will be necessary, as shown throughout the analysis.

As a means to measure how public resource commitments relate to secondary school access rates, Fig. 2.3 crosses these two variables for 49 African countries

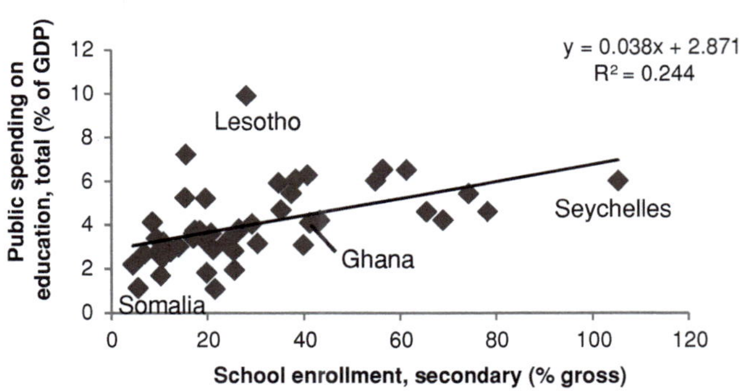

Fig. 2.3 African comparison of public spending on education and secondary school enrolment, 1970–2009 average.
Source Author's illustration based on data from World Development Indicators.
Note Public spending on education (as a share of GDP) and gross secondary school enrolment rates reflect country averages between 1970 and 2009 in order to smooth out annual fluctuations. Sudan has been omitted as a significant outlier due to incomplete data over all years

with available data over the period 1970–2009. The regression line shows that if a country spends one percent more on public education (as a share of GDP), this is correlated with an average increase of gross secondary school enrolment by about 25 %. Near to the African average, public spending on education in Ghana averaged 4.1 % of GDP over this period while the gross enrolment rate was 41.2 % at the secondary school level.

National Development Strategy and Education Policy

Human resource development is a central pillar in Ghana's Growth and Poverty Reduction Strategy. Establishing appropriate policies and strategies, on which actions and interventions are based, is a vital component in enabling Ghanaians to acquire higher levels of education. Within the 'Growth and Poverty Reduction Strategy' (GPRS II) outlined in 2006, the Government of Ghana lays down four main pillars needed for the country's development:

- Continued macroeconomic stability;
- Accelerated private sector-led growth;
- Vigorous human resource development;
- Good governance and civic responsibility (NDPC 2005).

"The most important lesson of contemporary economic history [and] the single most crucial key to the attainment of economic success", as stated by the government within the GPRS II, "is the educational quality of a nation's work force" (NDPC 2005, p. vi). Human resource development is an area recognised as the focal point of strategy and the centre of domestic priorities within the national development strategy (ibid.).

Government sets the ambitious target of 'free, compulsory, universal basic education'. The Education Strategic Plan (ESP) 2010–2020, which is the main policy document of the Ministry of Education (2009), outlines the strategic policy targets and goals of the education sector for the near- and medium-term. One policy stands out: 'Free, Compulsory, Universal Basic Education' (FCUBE) which aims to make schooling free of charge and compulsory for all 4–15-year-old children in Ghana (i.e. all children of preschool, primary and lower secondary age). With democratic rule via the 1992 Constitution coming back to Ghana on the 7th of January 1993 under President Rawlings, the strategy goal of education was laid down in article 38: "The Government shall [...] draw up a programme for implementation within the following ten years for the provision of free, compulsory and universal basic education" (Government of Ghana 1992). Four years later, the 'fcuBE' process (1996–2005) began to be carried out ('fcuBE' is abbreviated in lowercase throughout the analysis to emphasis its serious implementation constraints). For one, basic education is still not 'free' as for example the average family pays US$57.40 (GH¢52.81 at 2006 exchange rates) per primary student annually based on 2005/2006 GLSS data (for uniforms, transportation, lunches etc.) and accrues opportunity costs to send their children to school.[1] Second, it is still not fully 'compulsory' as field research conducted for this analysis in 2010 indicates that it is common practice for no action to be taken by law enforcement when children are not in school and instead, for example, selling goods on the street or assisting their family on the farm. Third, it is still not 'universal' as 20 % of children aged 4–15 (16.3 % aged 6–11) are out of school in the academic year 2008/2009 based on GDHS data calculations. In sum, there remain large gaps between the government's key policy objective in basic education and tangible signs of its achievement.

Despite policy shortcomings, attracting out-of-school children appears policy-driven. Policy has proven critical to bring educationally excluded children into the system given that success in attracting hundreds of thousands of children into schools since 2004/2005 can be attributed to policies such as the capitation grant scheme adopted in the same academic year (discussed later). Over the period 2004–2008, the number of out-of-school children is estimated to have reduced by almost half a million, from about 1.33 to 0.88 million children (World Bank EdStats). However, while the sector yielded accelerated growth in primary net enrolment at 17 % over the period 2004/2005–2006/2007, it has lost its momentum as primary net enrolment growth dropped to −2 % by 2009/2010 based on calculations here of administrative data. Chapter 8 covering policy options tackles the question of identifying innovative policy instruments and reforms to widen educational opportunities and increase the effectiveness and efficiency of public spending.

Educational Effects on Political Development in Ghana

While the political environment influences the education sector, education is in turn essential to consolidate Ghana's democratic gains. Nationally-representative data provided by the Afrobarometer (2008) is analysed in the following which is an independent research initiative and regarded as one of the most renowned in assessing the socio-political atmosphere in African states. Table 2.2 crosses data on levels of education of Ghanaians with their political values. Only about half of Ghanaians without schooling (55.7 %) strongly reject military rule, which has played a significant role in Ghanaian politics in the recent past (e.g. under President Rawlings), compared to about four out of five people who have tertiary education (82.6 %). One's support for democracy, likewise, tends to increase as one climbs up the educational ladder. In terms of political participation, data calculations show that people with secondary schooling are almost twice as likely to have made one or more complaints to local government officials and those with university education are about four times more likely to have done so compared to people without any formal schooling. The educational effect remains similar in

[1] Unless other sources are explicitly cited, the author's calculations of exchange rate conversions used throughout the analysis vary by annual averages from US$1.00 per GH¢0.92 (new Cedis) in 2006 and 2007, GH¢1.05 in 2008, GH¢1.49 in 2009 to GH¢1.45 in 2010 (Ghanaweb 2011).

Table 2.2 Educational profile of Ghanaians by various political values and behaviours, 2008

	Political values and beliefs					Political participation		Total
	Strongly reject one-party rule	Strongly reject military rule	Support democracy	Agree very strongly in questioning actions of leaders vs. respecting authority	Agree very strongly in people speaking minds vs. govt. suppressing expression	Made complaint to local government officials at least once	Voted in the last elections	
No formal schooling	49.0	55.7	75.1	27.3	44.7	8.1	88.1	24.6
Some or completed primary	61.2	55.9	78.7	30.2	48.7	7.9	81.1	40.5
Some or completed secondary	66.7	64.3	80.1	39.6	62.5	14.6	73.8	32.7
Some or completed university+	73.9	82.6	87.0	60.9	73.9	31.8	95.7	2.2
Total	60.3	59.2	78.4	33.2	52.8	10.7	80.8	100
Number of respondents	620	609	807	342	543	106	831	1,029

Source Author's calculations based on data from Afrobarometer 2008
Note Some or completed university also includes post graduates

terms of having made a complaint to a local government official, when disaggregating the data for differences in location (rural/urban) and wealth (measured as ownership/non-ownership of household goods like a car or motorcycle), while in contrast males—irrespective of their educational level—are much more likely than females to have made a complaint.

An explanation is that schooling, which aims to mediate reading, writing, arithmetic and analytical thinking skills, can promote democratic values and influence political participation and polity through its capacity to instil higher literacy rates, to help make better-founded decisions and to increase levels of income, as shown later in this analysis.

Conclusion: Political Environment

Stability, funding and policy are three political factors helping to shape the education sector's enabling environment. This chapter analysed how political variables like stability influence human and economic development, and especially the pathways through which they affect the education sector. Data over the past several decades reveal that changes in the political environment—from political will to specific policies—appear important in influencing Ghana's economic growth, levels of overall government expenditure and education spending as well as school enrolments during this period. While a stable and willing government in Ghana has been a fundamental condition for tax collection, tax revenue is in turn a prerequisite for public resource spending which is a central policy tool of the government to stimulate growth and invest in education, through which levels of schooling and skills development are influenced.

Political stability since 1982, when President Rawlings came to power, helped to influence the educational landscape in Ghana, but stronger democratic institutions especially during the 2000s appear to have been associated with even greater effects on the education sector. The acquisition of human resources can partly be traced back to political commitment and to large shares of education expenditure especially over the late 2000s at about 30 % of total public spending based on EMIS data, as the government has the principal role of investing in education. The sector also has a preferential position within the government's development strategy framework which has likely positively influenced the high resource allocation to the sector and helped to make significant progress towards national and international education targets. Overall, it appears that while political stability contributed to more stable and larger flows of education resources over the past decades, funding—although vital—is not sufficient in driving greater educational opportunities, which will remain contingent on effective policy instruments and organisations, as Chap. 8 later illustrates. Challenges remain and fully attaining a number of policy objectives will be difficult, most notably free, compulsory and universal basic education.

While promoting political stability may not be the strongest driver in improving educational access and outcomes in the country (relative to many other investment types), it remains important for the education sector's development. In turn, data evidence suggests that education can be critical in consolidating Ghana's political institutions. Thus, the implied finding is that political factors have as valid a place in studies on education development as they do in studies on economic development. Since increased levels of education and skills in Ghana are contingent on many non-education specific factors, some of which are macroeconomic, better understanding these empirical linkages as well is important for national policy planners and makers—this is the content of the ensuing chapter.

Chapter 3
Macroeconomics: Skills, Diversification, Economic Structure and Growth

Favourable macroeconomic conditions and political stability together with improved levels of education have all helped to contribute towards solid economic growth in Ghana over the period 2000–2008 at an annual average rate of 5.3 %, beyond any historical highs based on World Development data. This chapter sheds light on the inter-locking relationships between education, skills development, economic structure, diversification and growth in Ghana. It begins by analysing cross-country data to assess economic growth's linkages with educational spending and attainment. It then examines the extent to which an individual's educational profile influences their employment type and the country's overall economic structure. It explores how the economy's reliance on natural capital can trigger fluctuations in public revenue and education spending and helps to crowd out human resources. In turn, it looks at how increased enrolment in secondary schooling and greater school-life expectancy can help improve agricultural productivity and promote skills diversification.

Interconnections Between Economic Growth and the Education Sector

Two very common measures of education are discussed here considering their association with Ghana's track record on economic growth: (1) the share of government spending on education and (2) school-life expectancy. Cross-country correlation analysis in the following is largely based on previous work looking at these patterns in the 1980s and 1990s by Gylfason and Zoega (2003).

It is important that a government's emphasis on economic growth does not overcrowd public policy and lead to limited resource allocation to social sectors such as education and health and to poverty reduction. This is not the case in Ghana with (as mentioned) nearly one-third of current government expenditure allocated to education. While this large share of public spending on education is determined by the government, the overall amount of public spending is almost entirely established by the magnitude of the economy. That trends in the size of the public resource envelope tend to reflect trends in GDP growth is confirmed in Fig. 2.1 analysing patterns in Ghana since 1960.

A. Krauss, *External Influences and the Educational Landscape*,
SpringerBriefs in Economics, DOI: 10.1007/978-1-4614-4936-2_3,

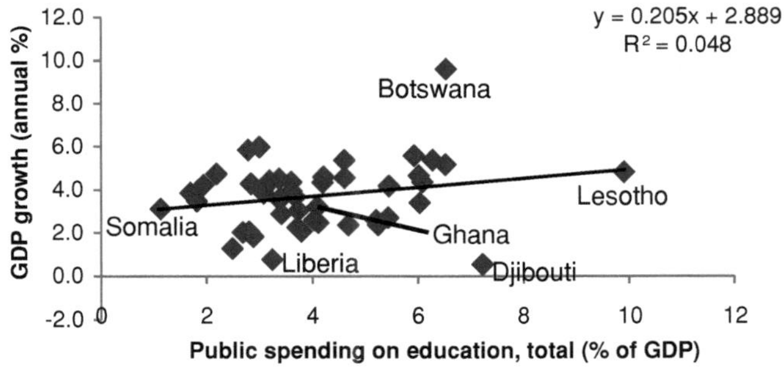

Fig. 3.1 African comparison of economic growth and public spending on education, 1970–2009 average
Source Author's illustration based on data from World Development Indicators
Note Two country outliers have been omitted, Sudan and Equatorial Guinea, due to incomplete data over all years. Analysing the average over a longer period, as indicated above, is helpful to blend out yearly fluctuations in these indicators

A 1 % rise in annual GDP correlates to a 5 % rise in education spending. Government commitment to education, measured here by the average public spending on education over the period 1970–2009 (to smooth out fluctuations over time), has been lower than 2 % of GDP in Nigeria (1.9), Guinea (1.8), Chad (1.7) and Somalia (1.3), while highest in Botswana (6.5), Djibouti (7.2) and Lesotho (9.9) based on calculations of World Development data. In Ghana, the respective share was 4.1 %. Figure 3.1 shows the relationship between economic growth and public education spending for 48 African countries with available data over the period 1970–2009. As the regression line indicates, an average rise in annual GDP growth of 1 % between African countries is related to a rise of about 5 % in government spending on education (as a share of GDP), although it is important to stress that this figure simply illustrates the cross-country correlation and is not to be interpreted as any kind of causality—which also applies to the following correlation analyses in this section.

5 years of more schooling for a country correlates to a 1.5 % rise in annual GDP. One way to measure the state of education development in a given country is by using school-life expectancy, which can indirectly reflect the sum of total education resources provided to the sector. A country's school-life expectancy is compared in Fig. 3.2 to economic growth rates across 52 African countries with available data using averages for the period 1970–2009. Each year of additional education among the population correlates to an average increase in annual economic growth of about 0.3 % so that in an average African country with 5 years more schooling the economy grew yearly at a rate of about 1.5 % higher over this period, measured in GDP, although there is a multitude of contributing factors. Although estimates of the effects of education on economic growth vary largely between studies and countries, the cumulative evidence seems to suggest that a high educational profile of the population is related to significant growth in GDP (see World Bank 2010c). A reason why additional years of education can potentially help to promote economic growth is by equipping the labour force with

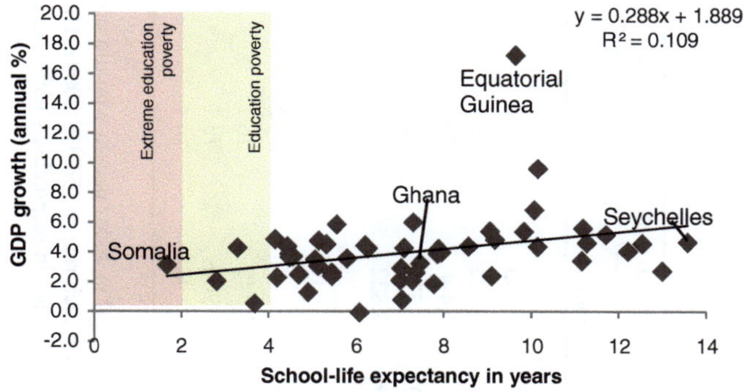

Fig. 3.2 African comparison of school-life expectancy and economic growth, 1970–2009 average *Source* Author's illustration based on data from Africa development indicators for school-life expectancy and from World Development Indicators for economic growth rates

reading and writing skills, possibly the principal objective of primary schooling, which are vital competencies in helping to boost productivity and development. "No country has ever achieved economic growth", as a World Bank (2002) study finds, "without reaching a critical threshold of about 40 % in its adult literacy rate". The literacy rate of people 15 years of age or older in Ghana is about 62 % based on administrative EMIS data for 2008.

Different types of employment mainly depend on one's level of acquired skills. Education also influences economic growth through its effects on the country's employment and economic structure, both of which are discussed in the following. Table 3.1 displays the dynamics of the occupational distribution in relation to levels of education, with employment defined in GDHS 2009 as 'currently working or working at any time during the last year preceding the survey' whether in the formal or informal sector. 84.1 % of men and 58.5 % of women without any schooling are employed in the agriculture sector. A reason for this is that agricultural labour generally demands no, or only minimal, schooling. The likelihood of being economically active in agriculture experiences, however, a strong descending trend at each higher level of education. Employment in professional, technical or managerial positions is a privilege nearly exclusively reserved for people with at least upper secondary education. Educationally deprived groups will therefore need to increase their stock of educational endowment to improve chances of securing better job options outside of agriculture.

There is an imbalance in the educational supply for and demand of the labour market. Upper secondary, technical and vocational education and training (TVET) and tertiary education appear to be largely supply-driven in Ghana. A study of Ghanaian graduates of higher education observed an unfulfilled supply of engineers, medical doctors, accountants and specialists in management and IT, all of which are vital areas for national development (Boateng and Ofori-Sarpong 2002). An excess supply of graduates was reported in subjects with easy admittance, above all in arts and humanities. These imbalances in the supply and demand of

Table 3.1 Distribution of the labour force by occupation and level of education, 2008/2009

	Professional/ technical/ managerial	Clerical	Sales and services	Skilled manual	Un-skilled manual	Agriculture	Missing	Total	Number of women/ men	Currently employed
Women										
No education	0.0	0.1	33.6	6.7	0.0	58.5	1.0	100	945	88.0
Primary	0.5	0.0	54.2	11.1	0.2	33.0	0.9	100	803	79.2
Lower sec.	1.0	0.3	62.1	14.2	0.1	20.7	1.7	100	1,496	70.8
Upper sec.+	27.4	11.0	48.7	7.8	0.5	2.7	1.8	100	575	62.7
Total	4.6	1.8	51.4	10.7	0.2	29.9	1.4	100	3,822	74.8
Men										
No education	0.5	2.1	3.7	8.4	0.0	84.1	1.2	100	527	96.3
Primary	1.7	6.7	8.5	20.4	0.3	58.5	4.0	100	483	76.5
Lower sec.	3.1	13.1	10.8	30.1	1.2	35.9	5.9	100	1,349	76.1
Upper sec.+	35.1	7.6	21.3	17.4	1.8	12.7	4.1	100	908	73.1
Total	11.4	8.8	12.2	21.6	1.0	40.6	4.3	100	3,276	79.7

Source Calculations based on GDHS

Note Shares refer to Ghanaians 15–49 years of age. Currently employed is defined as having done work in the past 7 days and includes people who did not work in the past 7 days but who are regularly employed and were absent from work for leave, illness, vacation or any other such reason (GDHS 2009). The share of the labour force involved in unskilled manual labour is lower than would be expected which might reflect some stigma in respondents identifying with this type of occupation university graduate labour have at least three adverse effects. First, they help to promote higher unemployment rates among graduates, as shown in Table 3.1. Secondly and consequently, they reduce the efficiency and effectiveness of government investment in higher education. And finally they deprive national development efforts of critical drivers (ibid.). In 2007/2008, 37.7 % of university students were registered in disciplines related to science and technology based on EMIS data. Policy may help to drive improvements, as the Ministry of Education (2010) has set the ambitious target of increasing this share to 60 % by the year 2020. Increased engagement of industry and employers in developing education policy would be helpful to improve the market relevance of upper secondary, TVET and tertiary institutions. A central challenge in Ghana, as the World Bank (2009b) notes, is to move towards higher value-added production and provision of services by investing more in relevant skills, technology and higher education. Further evidence of the large gap and unmet demand in trained and highly educated Ghanaians is provided in the data analysis within Chap. 6 that reveals very high rates of return to education, incremental at each level, and shows that employers pay tertiary degree holders 28.7 times the amount that they pay those who have no schooling (Table 6.3).

Despite the tertiary gross enrolment rate steadily increasing to reach 9.7 % by the academic year 2008/2009 (EMIS data), the share falls short for a country that aspires to enhance its competiveness and that has recently attained middle-income status, evidenced by country experiences across sub-Saharan Africa. These enrolment levels are far from optimal, as tertiary gross enrolment in high-income countries averaged 70.4 % in 2008, based on World Development data. The respective share for low-middle-income countries, the group in which Ghana falls as of late 2010, is 18.6 % (ibid.).

The Economic Structure and Agricultural Dependency Helps Crowd Out Human Capital

The economy's current structure contributes towards reduced public spending. In analysing (1) the corresponding shares of the Ghanaian labour force active in agriculture, industry or services and (2) the contributions of these respective sectors to GDP, it is possible to assess the potential effects of fluctuations in these indicators on available public resources. These two indicators also offer a possible illustration—although imperfect—of the degree of the economy's overall competitiveness. Together industry and services account for two-thirds (66.5 %) of measured GDP (Table 3.2), although only 44 % of the labour force, while most Ghanaians (56 %) are employed in agriculture-related activities. In Northern Ghana over 70 % of the population have agricultural livelihoods (GLSS 2005/2006 data). With agriculture accounting for 33.5 % of the country's GDP (World Development data), Ghana has a long way to go to shift away from its strong agricultural reliance, what is often seen as the most striking structural transformation from a developing to a developed country (see Ray 1998). The high

Table 3.2 Agriculture, industry and services in Ghana: output and growth in 2008

	Value added (constant 2000 USD, in billions)	Share of GDP (value added)	Annual share of growth (value added)
Agriculture	2.3	33.5	5.1
Industry	2.2	25.3	8.1
Services	3.2	41.2	8.6
National total	7.7	100	7.3

Source Data based on World Development Indicators

share of GDP in agriculture contributes to greater volatility in overall economic output (due largely to price fluctuations) and therefore greater volatility in the amount of public funding available for education. Moreover, as most Ghanaian workers are subsistence farmers and thus consume most of their labour output, their potential contribution to tax revenue is limited. Tax collection is a burden mainly falling on the share of the population working in the present formal sector: largely on industry and services, but also natural resource exports like cocoa and gold. It is important to emphasise that the rate at which the country increases its agricultural productivity in the short- and medium-term and reduces the sector's importance in overall GDP and the large shares of subsistence farmers in the longer term will strongly determine the rate at which the domestic tax base increases, and thus growth in available educational spending (see Krauss 2011).

In Ghana, a country richly endowed with natural resources, the economy depends strongly on exports of cocoa as the world's second largest producer and those of gold as one of the leading producers but also timber, manganese ore, diamonds, aluminium, bauxite, horticulture, tuna and—as of late 2010—oil (Chandra and Osorio-Rodarte 2007). Ghana is the seventeenth most agriculturally dependent economy out of 153 countries with available data between 2004 and 2008. The country's share of agricultural output at one-third of GDP is much higher than even a number of sub-Saharan countries such as Botswana (1.9), South Africa (3.3), Djibouti (3.9), Republic of Congo (4.0), Cape Verde (8.7), Namibia (9.1) and others (World Development data).

Agriculture's importance in the economy seems to decrease at a threshold of secondary enrolment at about 60 %. A strong adverse correlation is observed among countries reliant on agriculture and the share of student enrolment in secondary schooling, a major reason for which is likely the overall low demand for trained and skilled labour in those countries. Crossing data presented in Fig. 3.3 on the share of GDP in value added agriculture with gross secondary enrolment rates reveals that none of the 15 countries with a share of agriculture below 1.7 % of GDP has a gross secondary enrolment rate below 82 %, while none of the 15 countries with a share of agriculture above 34 % of GDP has a gross secondary enrolment rate above 50 %. From this international comparative perspective, the likelihood that productivity gains in agriculture take place and the size of the sector's contribution to the economy decreases appears high after reaching a threshold of about 60 % in gross secondary enrolment (Fig. 3.3). In Ghana, gross enrolment is only 54.1 % in secondary schooling. An average increase in a country's gross

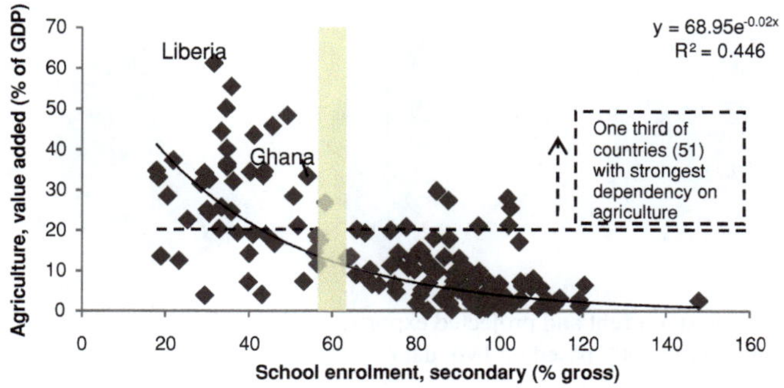

Fig. 3.3 International comparison of secondary enrolment rate and value added in agriculture, 2008 or closest year
Source Author's illustration based on data from World Development Indicators
Note Data refers to latest year between 2004 and 2008

secondary enrolment rate by 3 % is associated with an average decline in value added agriculture of about 1 % of GDP, although multiple factors contribute to this correlation. As the gross enrolment rate in secondary schooling nonetheless nears 100 %, a country generally acquires the prerequisite skills-base to foster increased agricultural efficiency, and then for the labour surplus to incrementally shift away from agriculture and move towards stronger manufacturing and services sectors. Widening access to market-relevant education at tertiary levels will likely only contribute to this economic transition. The degree to which this shift takes place will in turn influence the demand for a labour force with increasingly higher levels of secondary and superior education, as agricultural activities generally require minimal formal schooling.

In line with these findings, among the 40 African countries with available data the likelihood that an economic transition away from agriculture takes place (measured as a reduced share of GDP in agriculture) is high after reaching a threshold of about 10 years of education among the population based on calculations of World Development data for 2008 or closest year. In Ghana, school-life expectancy averaged 9.3 years in 2008. Likewise, cross-country evidence of the 146 countries with available data suggests that a strong natural resource sector (measured by the percentage of GDP in agriculture) is strongly and negatively associated with higher shares of public spending on education (ibid.).

It is important to take into account that since the majority of Ghanaians are employed in agriculture (GLSS 2005/2006 data), education development can be hindered because of the lack of possibilities to apply acquired knowledge and skills outside of the agriculture sector. On the one hand, until Ghana therefore finds viable means to diversify its economy, the formal education sector may not be able to completely fulfil its function of mediating relevant skills to children, youth and young adults. On the other hand, chances of increased economic diversification can be amplified by widening their educational opportunities and market-relevant knowledge base.

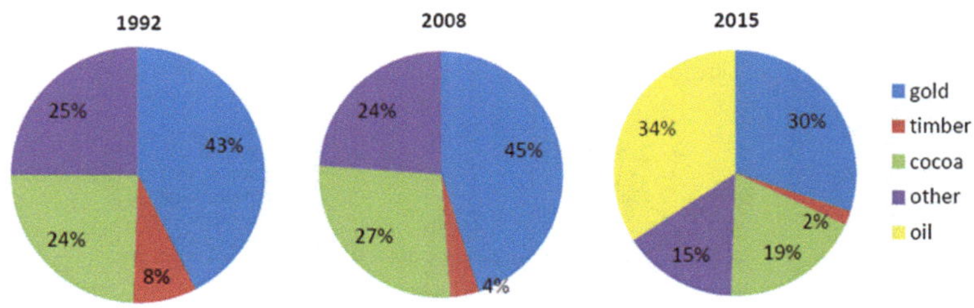

Fig. 3.4 Ghana's past, current and projected exports, 1992–2015
Source Moss and Young 2009 based on IMF data

A wealth of natural capital can help to crowd out human capital. GDHS data for 2008/2009 indicate that most people active in the primary labour sector such as agriculture, fishery, mining and forestry have either no schooling or only primary education which hinders their possibilities to explore other forms of more gainful employment. Ghana's abundant natural capital and high agricultural labour intensity have implications on the schooling system to the effect that there may be fewer incentives to make investments in higher levels of education, thereby constraining skills development, technological advancements and thus national development. In part due to the country's agriculture sector being employed mainly by small-scale farmers, who tend to have low shares of human capital and low productivity on the farm, this can be viewed as the primary cause of having both low-input as well as producing low-output in agriculture (Govindasamy et al. 2006). As long as natural resources are responsible for the vast majority of exports in Ghana (Fig. 3.4), much of the labour force will be stuck in low-skill intensive primary-commodity industries, which can help to trigger potential Dutch disease effects and are commonly a main cause of reduced export growth and lower per capita levels of income in the country (Chandra and Osorio-Rodarte 2007).

Cocoa and gold continue to drive the economy but a by-product is the low levels of public revenue and a very low demand on skilled labour. Cocoa and gold are the two major exports that together have been a central driving force of the economy for more than a century (Chandra and Osorio-Rodarte 2007). Ghana, known as the Gold Coast for the British colonialists, remains sub-Saharan Africa's second-largest producer of the metal following South Africa, while ninth-largest in the world. Gold exports represented US$2.2 billion in 2008 but this translated into only US$116 million in taxes and royalties accrued from mining companies or about 4 % of total tax (The Economist 2010). In terms of cocoa, Ghana exported between 20 and 25 % of the world's supply in the mid-1990s (Glewwe and Ilias 1996). As prices of cocoa (like gold) are subject to external shocks, however, the core of the economy remains vulnerable. Fluctuations in cocoa and gold prices have affected GDP growth more so during periods when prices deflated than during those when prices increased. For instance, the price of cocoa fell by nearly 50 % over the 2 year period 1998–2000 while GDP fell by 20 %. As commodity prices increased during the period 2001–2005, growth in GDP remained, however, low (Chandra and Osorio-Rodarte 2007).

There is some uncertainty if Ghana can rise above the 'oil curse' and re-direct oil revenue to domestic development. Ghana recently made oil discoveries off its coast, and reserves are estimated at 490 million barrels of oil (World Bank 2009b). Production has begun as of December 2010. It would nonetheless be surprising if the advent of oil revenue does not lead to some degree of increased volatility in government revenue as experienced in a number of oil-producing countries. The IMF (2009) predicts that the government will earn about US$1.3 billion annually in oil revenues for the coming 2 decades, while taking into account that Ghana had a 13.9 billion dollar economy (GNI) in 2007 based on World Development data. Since reserves are relatively small in terms of their contributing share of the country's GDP compared to other oil-producers, it is unlikely that they have the potential to bring fundamental economic change (Moss and Young 2009). While governments of some countries with large oil reserves have commonly been less inclined in the long-run to make large-scale public investments in the education sector given their limited market demand for a well skilled labour force, human development in Ghana has been much more sustainable than in some older oil-producing countries within Africa such as Equatorial Guinea, Sudan and Angola. In sum, oil—if managed well—may help to diversify the government's revenue base in the short-term but it is questionable if it will have similar effects in the long-term especially on diversifying the country's human resources.

Debt relief and international development assistance can increase public resources. There are indications that the Government of Ghana has nearly maximised its potential of (an already limited) tax collection, especially given the economy's large informal sector and since 53.6 % of Ghanaians live on less than $2 (PPP) a day (2008 World Development data). From the viewpoint of the public resource pool, alleviating foreign debt has been an effective means to ensure increased public resources and investments in human resource development, as primary health and education generally receive all savings accrued through debt relief (Oseil and Quartey 2001). International assistance can also help to fill financial gaps in the supply of funding for education. But as a relatively aid-dependent country (accounting for 8 % of GDP and 6 % of education expenditure in the late 2000s based on EMIS data) Ghana needs to begin exploring more sustainable strategies, especially as the country recently crossed the threshold into middle income status and external grant funding will therefore be minimised and eventually eliminated in the medium-term.

Conclusion: Macroeconomic Environment

Macroeconomic changes interact with the supply of and the demand for education. The supply is determined for instance by fluctuations in the amount of public revenue available for the provision of education. The demand is affected for instance by the country's employment and economic structure that largely require labourers with limited schooling. This chapter began by exploring economic growth, finding that it is strongly associated with education, using different indicators reflecting educational inputs (public spending on the sector) and outcomes (years of schooling). Annual economic growth in Ghana over the period 2000–2008 averaged 5.3 %, beyond all historical highs (World Development data), while public spending allocated to education reached about 8 % of GDP during this period (administrative EMIS data), beyond all historical highs. Economic growth has been identified as one of the most important external influences shaping the educational landscape in Ghana.

Ghana's strong natural resource sector contributes to lower demand on education as well as a volatile and more limited public resource pool. Findings show that Ghana's current economic structure adversely affects the education system, with the natural resource sector—responsible for nearly all exports and most labourers—helping to crowd out human resources because of the lack of possibilities to apply acquired knowledge and skills outside of the natural resource sector. It is unlikely that the advent of oil exports will alleviate this situation, but will rather likely only aggravate it. Cross-country data analysis here indicates a high likelihood that the importance of the agriculture sector in the economy decreases after reaching a threshold of gross secondary enrolment at about 60 % (with gross secondary enrolment at 54.1 % in Ghana for 2008) or about 10 years of education among the population (with 9.3 years of education in Ghana for the same year). One conclusion therefore is that the country is nearing a critical point for economic transformation if greater investments and efficiency gains in agriculture are made. The rate at which the Ghanaian labour force raises agricultural productivity—to which increased schooling and skills contribute—in the short- and medium-term and shifts away from the agriculture sector in the longer term will likely strongly determine the rate at which: (1) potential fluctuations in public revenue reduce due to diminished shocks from volatile commodity prices, (2) the need for greater education services rises as the natural resource sector only needs a limited share of highly skilled workers, and (3) the domestic tax base increases due to fewer subsistence workers and thus growth in available education spending increases.

GDHS data analysis shows that different types of employment are highly correlated with one's level of acquired education and skills. Ghana's labour and export diversification will therefore be conditional on its skills diversification, with the speed of scaling up exports in further sectors largely dependent on the speed of Ghanaians' capacity to overcome scarce educational capital of diverse technological skills. There remains, however, an excess supply of graduates in arts and humanities, for instance, while only 37.7 % of enrolments in public universities were in science and technology in 2007/2008 based on administrative EMIS data, although a target is set for 60 % by 2020. The overall results justify improved policy and reinforce the necessity for more targeted inputs and improved outputs in research, skills and innovation in order to foster diversification and improve the country's competitiveness.

Finally, the overall amount available in the public resource envelope is largely established by the magnitude of the economy, while the government establishes the share of public spending allocated towards education (at almost one-third of total public expenditure), so that sustaining levels of spending in education and improving levels of education in Ghana will continue to largely rely on how rapidly the economy grows and to what extent there is a continuum of political stability and commitment in coming years. The current high share of education spending suggests that the Government of Ghana views the sector as possibly the central driving force for skills and technology development, economic diversification and a main motor for growth. At the same time, however, it is important to take into account that improvements at the national level, in both macroeconomic and political variables, generally only lead to greater educational attainment if they are directed towards underlying influencers of educational improvements at the individual, household, community and regional level.

Part II
The Geographic, Health, Economic and Demographic Environment for Education Development

A central message from the previous two chapters is that if Ghana did not have a relatively stable political and macroeconomic environment over the past two to three decades, which is commonly seen as a prerequisite for national development and is less common in the sub-Saharan region, available resources for and improvements in education and skills development would have been further constrained. Taking this constraining or enabling environment at the macro level into account, the following four chapters evaluate the interactions of various individual, household, community and regional characteristics (also some national factors) with educational development in Ghana.

As opposed to the preceding two chapters which largely examine national, aggregate data, the subsequent four chapters focus largely on analysing household survey data to establish which non-education specific variables are important in pushing and pulling school access and outcomes in Ghana, especially for children and youth. This is done from four perspectives by analysing the geographic, health, economic and demographic environment for education development. To the extent possible, the effects of different levels of education on a number of factors at these levels are also assessed.

Chapter 4
Geography and the Tale of Two Ghanas: The North–South Divide

Physical geography matters for development. Accordingly, development trends in Ghana are largely shaped by its geographic circumstances. Ghana—also West Africa for that matter—is not located on one of the major global trade routes, contributing to less favourable export market conditions. Many communities in Ghana are located in remote areas and are sparsely populated, raising the costs of basic social service delivery and infrastructure development. Most tropical zones, and those with higher precipitation levels such as the forest belt, have ecological conditions that favour mortal diseases such as malaria. The North (or Northern Ghana, which incorporates the Upper West, Upper East and Northern regions) has an arid environment conducive to a higher prevalence of drought and its population is known to live under harsher environmental and agricultural conditions.

Economic development in Ghana cannot be separated from the country's natural resources (as previously indicated cocoa and gold account for the vast majority of exports, to which oil has begun contributing). Likewise, the country's human development is fundamentally dependent on geographic conditions. This chapter examines the scope and nature of the large disparities in educational development across the urban–rural divide, between regions and within communities. It evaluates the role that low population density and school distance play in shaping educational opportunities. The education and skills gap separating the North of the country from the South is a pressing developmental problem and of particular interest in this analysis. It is argued here that one of the largest challenges in the education sector facing the government today lies in the improvement of the provision of services and the development of incentive packages aimed at Northerners. Given that Ghana aspires to attain universal basic education, progress and inevitably achievement will be almost entirely conditional on how effective the government but also non-governmental stakeholders are in concentrating these efforts on the marginalised North.

The North–South Educational Divide

Taken as a whole, possibly the most remarkable characteristic within the Ghanaian development context is the geographic divide between the North and South of the country. This divide impacts nearly all sectors and nearly all development

A. Krauss, *External Influences and the Educational Landscape*, SpringerBriefs in Economics, DOI: 10.1007/978-1-4614-4936-2_4,

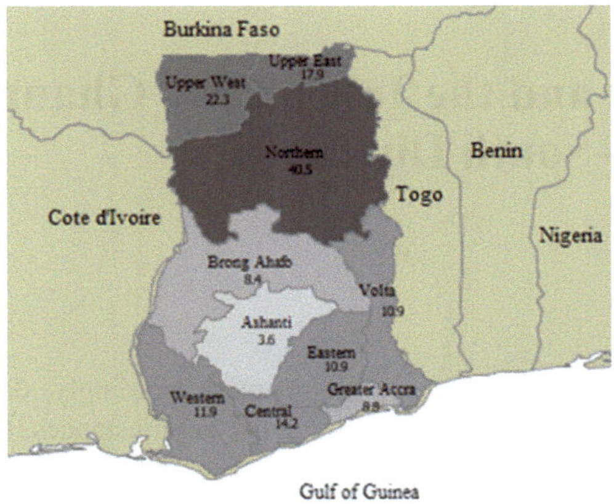

Map 4.1 Political-administrative regions in Ghana and the educational deprivation of the North: share of 6–14-year olds who did not attend school in the academic year 2008/09
Source Author's illustration based on calculations of data from GDHS (all geographic maps throughout the analysis are made by the author using gvSIG map making software)

indicators. There is no exception for the education sector. Looking at the gap between these two parts of the country is therefore essential when trying to better understand why many children and young adults have no schooling or are less educated. Map 4.1, which illustrates the ten political–administrative regions in Ghana, indicates that the North lags far behind the rest of the country in terms of basic school attendance. With 15.6 % of all Ghanaian children 6–14 years of age not attending school in the country in 2008/09, the share in the North (28.4 %) is over three times higher than in the South (9.3 %).

A number of geographic factors are interconnected and help to impede educational access and outcomes. In the North, where many inter-locking variables related to lower human and economic development reinforce each other, population density that is 3.6 times lower than in the South makes delivering education services more expensive and distances to school slightly farther which in turn can increase transportation costs to go to school. In 2010, 39.9 people per square kilometre lived in the North against 142.4 people in the South (national average of 100.4). Although the North accounts for 41 % of the country's land mass, it is only inhabited by 16 % of its population or 19 % of the primary-age population (6–11-year olds) based on Ghana Statistical Service data crossed with EMIS data for 2010. But, its population is not just widely and sparsely dispersed, it also must cope with climate stress that continues to intensify in this part of the country (World Bank 2010d). This, coupled with lower soil fertility and more unpredictable water and resource availability, generates lower agricultural productivity and output than in southern areas, and leads to food insecurity being more precarious in the North (ibid.). As most Northerners rely on subsistence farming, the situation is aggravated and it is this dependency which increases the opportunity costs of sending children to school, as statistical analysis in Chap. 6 shows. It is also in the North where households are not only more socio-economically deprived but also have higher fertility, which combined can help limit households' capacity to afford school fees for all children. With the compounding constraint imposed by basically being 'land-locked' due to poor infrastructure, Northern Ghana is the most physically isolated and least integrated part of the country. It is, however, not only geographically disadvantaged, but remains also politically disadvantaged, as it still does not receive the appropriate or necessary attention at the policy- and resource allocation-level.

The North has been and continues to be politically neglected. At the time of gaining independence, one secondary school existed in the North, the government secondary school in Tamale, in contrast to a long tradition of secondary schooling in the South (World Bank 2010d). Achieving equitable education opportunities in the North of the country, where not just schooling but also other social services had been nearly entirely ignored by the political elite during colonial times, has been a formidable challenge for recent governments. Today, resource allocation to the North continues to lag behind, at times far behind, as evidenced by the government not assuming full responsibility in (i) establishing equitable school infrastructure, (ii) delivering equitable human resources and (iii) allocating equitable financial resources. First, a spatial picture of the extent of the inequitable distribution of schools between the North and South is provided by crossing administrative EMIS data from 2008 on, for example, the number of secondary schools with the estimated 12–17-year-old population from 2010: 16.7 % of the 12–14-year-old population lives in the North, where 10.8 % of lower secondary schools are located, as the South has 83.3 % of the respective population and 89.2 % of the corresponding schools. In upper secondary, the North is home to 16.5 % of the 15–17-year-old population and 13.3 % of school facilities at this level, while the South has 83.5 % of the respective population and 86.7 % of the corresponding schools. Therefore, at the lower secondary level the population–school ratio is 1.5 in the North (with 1.0 meaning absolute equality) and 1.2 at the upper secondary level. Second, another way to measure the extent of Northern Ghana's continued political neglect is to evaluate the spatial distribution of school teachers relative to students across the country. For the academic year 2008/09, pupil teacher ratios in public primary schools are much higher in the Northern (45:1), Upper West (47:1) and Upper East (48:1) regions compared to all Southern regions and were particularly low in the Eastern (30:1) and Volta (30:1) regions based on EMIS data. Third, over the late 2000s nearly all of the Ministry of Education's budget is allocated to teacher salaries, 96 % in 2010 (EMIS data), which provides—given the findings above—an illustration of the inequitable distribution of government funding to the North.

The share of 18-year olds and above without completed primary schooling reduced from 50.3 to 43.4 % between 1993/94 and 2008/09 but progress has been spatially uneven. The subsequent increased levels of completed schooling—despite improvements in both the North and South—are geographically uneven, with the difference in the share of adults who have no schooling between the North and South having grown from 40.8 to 42.7 % over the same period (Table 4.1). In 2008/09, the North has over twice as many adults without any completed level of schooling and about twice as few upper secondary and tertiary graduates as the South. A finding of particular policy concern is that while the share of tertiary graduates increased in the South, it has stagnated at 1.1 % in the North which could be partly attributed to the high concentration of tertiary

Table 4.1 Levels of education among the adult population (18 years of age or older) by North–South divide, over the period 1993/94–2008/09

Highest level of completed education	1993/94				2008/09			
	North	South	Total	Number of observations	North	South	Total	Number of observations
None	82.9	42.1	50.3	5,261	73.9	31.2	43.4	10,670
Primary	4.5	12.1	10.6	1,108	7.3	12.2	10.8	2,654
Lower secondary	7.9	36.5	30.7	3,214	8.6	36.9	28.8	7,087
Upper secondary	3.6	7.3	6.6	689	9.1	17.2	14.9	3,674
Tertiary	1.1	2.0	1.8	187	1.1	2.5	2.1	506
Total	100	100	100	10,459	100	100	100	24,591

Source Author's calculations based on data from GDHS

Note As survey respondents have experienced several phases of restructuring of the education system over past decades, levels of education are classified here uniformly as follows: no education completed refers to individuals ranging from those without any schooling to those who may have reached class 5 but did not complete primary, while completing 6, 9, 12 and 16 years of schooling refers to completion of primary, low secondary, upper secondary and tertiary education, respectively

institutions in the South of the country and which may have implications on scaling up such institutions in the North.

Extreme education poverty, while nearly eradicated in the South, affects one quarter of Northern youth. A North–South profile of education poverty provided in Table 4.2 identifies various background characteristics of youth 15–19 years of age who are educationally most impoverished—applying the measurement of education poverty (less than 4 years of schooling) and extreme education poverty (less than 2 years of schooling) based on parameters established by UNESCO (2010). National averages hide very large disparities between Northerners and Southerners, insofar as 34.1 % of the North's population falling into this age group lives in education poverty (25.8 % in extreme education poverty) compared to only 9.3 % in the South (4.8 % in extreme education poverty). The likelihood for youth of this age to live in extreme education poverty is therefore five times greater in the North of the country. From a perspective of the very marginalised, 72.3 % of adolescent girls of this age are on average educationally poor if they live in the rural North within the bottom wealth quintile and in a household with three or more children under-5, whereas only 30 % are classified as such if they live in the South with the same background characteristics (data tabulations not shown in Table 4.2). In terms of the second MDG, while four out of five youth 15–19 years of age (80.0 %) have been able to complete a full course of primary schooling in the South, only about half have had the same opportunity in the North (53.2 %).

Analysing levels of education among the adult population (Table 4.1) provides an overview of the current skills market in Ghana and examining educational poverty among older adolescents (Table 4.2) offers insight into potential market shortages of knowledge and skills in the short-term. Subsequently, evaluating primary completion and then school participation (Fig. 4.1) helps to provide data-driven evidence of the future skills supply in the medium- and longer term, while disaggregating data along the North–South divide reveals large spatial gaps across the country.

Table 4.2 Share of youth aged 15–19 who are educationally impoverished and who are MDG-2 achievers in 2008/09, by North versus South

	Share of 15–19 year olds living in:						Share of 15–19 year olds who:			
	Extreme education poverty (less than 2 years of completed school)			Education poverty (less than 4 years of completed school)			Completed primary (6 or more years of completed school)			Number of observations of 15–19 year olds
	Total	North	South	Total	North	South	Total	North	South	
Total	11.4	25.8	4.8	17.1	34.1	9.3	71.5	53.2	80.0	4,842
Sex										
Male	9.8	23.2	3.2	16.4	33.1	8.1	71.4	53.2	80.4	2,456
Female	13.1	28.7	6.3	17.9	35.1	10.5	71.6	53.3	79.6	2,386
Location										
Rural	16.1	30.0	6.6	23.9	39.6	13.1	61.9	46.1	72.7	2,853
Urban	4.7	12.8	2.8	7.4	16.6	5.4	85.4	75.5	87.6	1,989
Wealth quintile										
Lowest	30.0	35.0	15.7	41.4	45.6	29.8	43.7	41.2	50.5	1,221
Second	9.6	17.9	6.4	16.1	25.2	12.7	68.3	58.8	71.9	948
Middle	5.5	11.9	4.1	10.1	16.3	8.8	77.3	73.1	78.2	913
Fourth	3.1	8.0	2.2	5.5	11.7	4.3	86.7	79.6	88.1	875
Highest	2.1	2.9	2.1	3.5	2.9	3.6	92.4	89.9	92.7	885
Number of children under-5 in household										
0	8.0	20.9	3.9	13.1	29.3	7.8	77.8	60.2	83.5	2,710
1	12.3	24.4	5.3	18.6	32.8	10.4	66.6	50.0	76.1	1,296
2	15.8	27.4	7.9	23.0	35.7	14.4	64.9	53.5	72.7	570
3 or more	32.3	48.2	7.7	38.7	54.9	13.5	46.2	33.3	66.4	266

Source Author's calculations based on data from GDHS

Note Wealth quintiles are determined by combining indicators of household income, expenditure and conditions, ranging from household ownership of consumer items like a television or a car to dwelling characteristics like sanitation facilities, source of water and type of flooring material (GDHS 2009)

Southerners have a strong comparative advantage to their Northern counterparts, with no region in the North surpassing 90 % primary completion rates in 2008/09 while all Southern regions did. A very revealing finding from the data analysis is that the Western region has—as the first region in the country—already achieved universal primary completion among its 17-year-old population, illustrating that it should be possible for other regions as well (based on calculations of GDHS data).

Although multiple influences contribute to the cross-regional disparities (as the analysis later shows), it is worth stressing that households in the North are more likely to weigh the rewards of primary schooling relative to the probability of being able to continue onto further levels of schooling. An explanation for this is that increased rates of return to schooling, particularly in the North, begin after completing at least lower secondary, as household heads 15 years of age or older in the North with lower secondary education earn annually on average GH¢375 from employment compared to GH¢63 and GH¢77 for those with no schooling and primary education, respectively—based on data calculations in Table 6.3.

Ghana is on-track to achieve MDG-2 in a few Southern regions but it appears unlikely in the North. If efforts over the period 1993/94–2008/09 are sustained at the current rate (high) or at half the rate (low) using simple extrapolation, how long will it take for universal primary completion to be achieved? Even under the most hopeful of scenarios, some regions will take many decades to reach MDG-2 and, once reached, face new challenges in attaining universal basic education. Other regions, especially in the South, have the possibility to meet the goal by 2015: the Ashanti region for the 13-year-old population and the Central region for the 17-year-old population. At the same time, it is important to remember that trends are rarely linear as it is most difficult to reach the most marginalised (the last percentiles). This is also evidenced by some of the regions, which are close to universalising primary completion, showing signs of stagnation and even regression over this period—two examples are the Greater Accra and Eastern regions (based on calculations of GDHS data). This means that some low estimates may even be unlikely for some marginalised groups in society such as those who come from large families, are malnourished, involved in labour activities or a combination of these, as subsequent chapters illustrate.

It is evident, as these data findings confirm, that the education system in Ghana was largely designed half a century ago when students mainly stemmed from the elite urban South, and it has not yet fully adapted to the reality of providing universal basic schooling for Northern and Southern children alike. Regression analysis in Chap. 6 highlights these shortcomings and indicates that geographic location in the North is the strongest predictor in constraining school participation, with other factors like age, sex, household welfare and number of household members held constant (Table 6.6). In Fig. 4.1, descriptive evidence of these shortcomings is provided. School attendance rates for 11-year-old children, for example, are 22.2 % lower in the North compared to the South. Several other very interesting findings can be derived from the following figure. For one, if children in the North do not enrol into school by the age of about 10–12 they are likely to

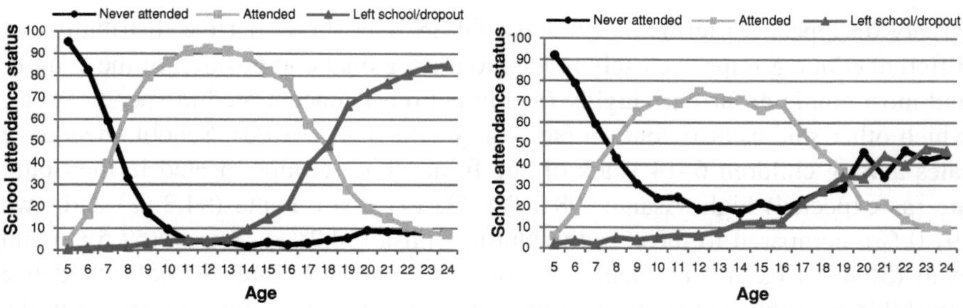

Fig. 4.1 School attendance status in the South (*left*) and North (*right*) by age of children and youth, for the academic year 2008/09
Source Author's illustration based on calculations of data from GDHS
Note Attendance rates also include those who may be repeating. Together, the three shares (never attended, attended and left school/dropout) total 100 % for each individual age. The figures are based on a survey sample of 14,362 children and youth for the South and 6,684 for the North

never go to school while this is not necessarily the case in the South. This is likely explained largely by the strong demand for child labour in the agriculturally-dependent North (Chap. 6). Second, the North lags far and consistently behind the South in terms of attendance rates up to the age of 19, when the share of Northerners going to school surpasses that of Southerners as a result of very late enrolment—i.e. some over-age youth trying to catch up. Third, significant shares of children are only entering school for the first time once they are between 8 and 12 years of age, when school participation hits its peak point. Two of the underlying reasons why children start school later than the official age are due to the need for young children to assist parents on the farm and due to stunting caused by malnutrition which gives parents the perception that their children may not be old or mature enough to go to school, as statistical analysis in subsequent chapters reveals. Late entry into the school system can jeopardise the schooling experience of young Ghanaians and contribute to higher levels of dropout as many leave school without graduating to enter early into the labour force (an issue elaborated on later in the analysis). It raises furthermore policy concerns about identifying effective means to ensure that the compulsory component of the fcuBE policy is *de facto* implemented through law enforcement officials. More importantly, as the decision to not send a child to school is possibly the most important in limiting a child's future opportunities, it would be interesting for policy planners to consider ways in which parents could possibly become sanctioned for their children's non-attendance, which would be feasible if, for example, a reformed capitation grant (conditional on school attendance) would target households as opposed to schools, a policy reform proposed in Chap. 8.

Residency in the North or South largely explains variations in education indicators among different ethnic and religious groups. Two variables which are not given much attention in this analysis are ethnicity and religion. This is because they, on their own, offer very little explanatory value in understanding inequitable education. Once variables for geographic location are included, differences largely disappear. In terms of ethnicity, GLSS data show that the distribution of different ethnic groups is closely related to the regional composition of the country and most ethnic groups are highly (nearly entirely) concentrated in specific areas, which other studies also confirm (see e.g. World Bank 2010d). School attendance rates among children 6–14 years of age from ethnic groups located in the South are (as expected) high, Asante (98.5 %), Ga (97.0 %), Fante (94.2 %) and Ewe (91.0 %), compared to those in the North, Builsa (58.2 %), Kusasi (57.5 %) and Wali (56.8 %) based on calculations of GLSS 2005/06 data. School attendance for children of this age from these three ethnic groups that typically reside in the North but have migrated and are living in the South rises to 82.4 % for Builsa, 86.8 % for Kusasi and 83.3 % for Wali, although the size of these child populations in the South is very small relative to that in the North. School completion rates follow the same trends. It is also important to note that results for religious affiliation are similar to those for ethnic background. GLSS data calculations for 2005/06 confirm that the vast majority of Muslims live in the North and Christians in the South so that school attendance rates for children 6–14 years of age are (as expected) higher among Methodists (98.3 %) and Presbyterians (96.7 %) relative to Muslims (80.2 %). These results support the argument that observed ethnic and religious differences on specific education indicators almost entirely reflect the concentration of disadvantaged groups in the isolated North rather than intrinsic cultural norms. Other reasons why variables such as ethnicity or religion are not further analysed here are because field research and data analysis in this study suggest that deliberate marginalisation or discrimination along these lines does not seem to exist in Ghana but is explained historically by the political neglect of the North and its less favourable geographic conditions. Furthermore, results would have very limited policy relevance and any policy rooted in ethnic promotion would likely cause social stigma and could create ethnic tensions.

Rurality

About half of Ghanaians live in a rural area where school demand and supply are lower. One of the major explanations for the North–South educational gap is that almost four-fifths of Northerners (78.2 %) live in rural areas while only about half of Southerners (52.9 %) live in such areas based on calculations of GDHS data for 2008/09. One example of the urban–rural divide is that 50 % of students enrolled in the five oldest public universities, all of which are located in urban areas, come from only 5.8 % of all the public upper secondary schools (29 out of 493 respective schools) in the country, the vast majority of which are located in urban areas, based on EMIS data (World Bank 2011).

Figure 4.2 illustrates a common rural classroom in Ghana, and provides insight into the scarce infrastructural facilities facing some schools that are confronted with serious operational difficulties during the rainy season, and may even have to close at times, as primary participatory observations indicate. Basic service delivery for education within rural and remote areas is accompanied by a number of other constraints. For children, distances to school tend to be further. For schools, ensuring adequate facilities and the supply of water and functioning toilets has proven to be a serious challenge (as statistical analysis in Chap. 5 shows). For civil servants, particularly teachers, incentive packages are often not sufficient to retain them in hard-to-reach areas (see World Bank 2011). The Minister of Education validated this by stating that "most Ghanaian youth are not ready [willing] to serve in the critical areas, the rural areas, where their services are most needed". Year after year, a large number of newly trained teachers refuse postings in 'bush schools' within off-road rural settings and many of those teachers who accept a rural position request to be relocated to a school in an urban area or decide to abandon the occupation altogether, as a study revealed (EARC 2003).

There is a certain degree of 'state failure' in relation to public education provision, especially in rural areas. The Minister of Education noted that "by our constitution and laws regarding education, it is the responsibility of local government, [...] to provide the structures and even furnish the schools for the children [...]. Where either the local government defaults on this or central government hasn't got those large-scale programmes, [...] it takes a long time for those schools to make access to school readily available". This is where the private sector comes in and helps to fill gaps in service delivery. Free education is therefore not 'free' as evidenced by private sector expansion. The share of private schools in the country has risen rapidly to account for about one-fifth of all schools at the basic level by 2009/10 based on EMIS data. In terms of students, 19.5 % of kindergarten, 18.6 % of primary, 17.4 % of lower secondary, 10.8 % of upper secondary and 14 % of tertiary students were educated privately in the same academic year (EMIS data). More importantly, while for example about half of all public schools in upper secondary (48.6 %) were located in urban areas, this share was only 26.6 % for private schools, indicating that 73.4 % of all private schools at this level deliver services to those living in rural areas (World Bank 2011). Given the strong geographic distribution of private schools in rural areas (which are typically poor) coupled with the government's policy of 'free' education, it is possible to argue that there is a certain degree of state failure taking place in terms of public service delivery of education in Ghana.

Distance to School

A coherent education policy that ensures sufficient school infrastructure is a requirement for any effective education strategy. Once a minimum threshold in school facilities is met, the significance of such a policy diminishes, but such a minimum threshold has not yet been reached and school distance still constrains some pockets of children and youth in hard-to-reach areas and disproportionately affects the North. Based on the Core Welfare Indicators Questionnaire Survey, about 5 % of out-of-school children cited that commuting to school was too far, when questioned why they were not attending a primary school (GSS 2003).

Fig. 4.2 Classroom infrastructure deficiencies in a rural school in Ghana, 2010

22.5 % of primary students take at least 1 hour to get to and come home from school. For GLSS, respondents were asked, how much time is spent going to and from school daily, which partly reflects the geographic and economic costs of attending school and could be used as a proxy indicator of the need for additional school construction. Table 4.3 calculates the number of hours—up to 1 hour, up to 2 hours or over 2 hours—spent in going to and home from school daily for the share of the respective population attending a given class for the academic year 2005/06. It reveals that students in the North traverse overall somewhat longer distances to and from school than those living in the South, but the differences between these two parts of the country may not be as large as would be expected. Nonetheless, 18.7 % of preschoolers in the South, for example, take at least 1 hour to commute to and from school compared to 25.8 % of their counterparts in the North. Moreover, one in every ten lower secondary students in the North travels over 2 hours daily to and from school. This offers evidence of the strong motivation of these students to attend school even where the government may fall short—or fail—to provide sufficient school facilities and resources. Field research conducted for this analysis in 2010 with upper secondary students in the capital Accra indicates that distance is an influential factor in deciding on not to send children onto lower secondary school as possibilities to continue beyond this level tend to be reserved for the most privileged Table 4.3.

Four other points, which data in Table 4.3 do not capture, should be mentioned. First of all, even though analysis of school distances offers information on an underlying cause of spatial barriers for some pupils in the country, school proximity does not capture the effect of the price to attend school. Calculations of GLSS data for 2005/06 indicate that on average 6–7 % of annual household expenditure on education is used for school transportation, so that for example the average upper secondary student spent US$18.10 (GH¢ 16.65 at 2006 exchange rates) in that year. Second, as the vast majority of children and youth assist their parents with tasks at home before and/or after school, the need to travel longer distances to school can increase their opportunity costs and represent at times an indirect deterrent to pursue their schooling. Third, longer distances imply less time for homework and extracurricular learning. Finally, school proximity for out-of-school children—as data in Table 4.3 only reflect school attendees—is likely an even more serious issue.

Table 4.3 Share of students spending up to 1 hour, up to 2 hours or over 2 hours in going to and from school, 2005/06

	Total					South					North				
	0–59 min	60–119 min	120+ min	Total	Number of observations	0–59 min	60–119 min	120+ min	Total	Number of observations	0–59 min	60–119 min	120+ min	Total	Number of observations
Preschool	79.8	15.0	5.2	100	2,458	81.3	13.9	4.8	100	1,931	74.2	19.2	6.6	100	527
Primary	77.5	16.4	6.2	100	6,451	77.5	16.2	6.3	100	4,715	77.4	16.7	6.0	100	1,736
Lower secondary	73.3	19.6	7.1	100	1,923	73.8	19.6	6.5	100	1,561	70.4	19.6	10.0	100	362
Upper secondary	76.5	18.4	5.1	100	750	76.2	19.1	4.7	100	621	77.6	15.1	7.3	100	129
University	82.0	9.8	8.2	100	122	80.9	10.0	9.1	100	110	91.7	8.3	0.0	100	12
Other tertiary	54.3	14.3	31.4	100	35	60.0	13.3	26.7	100	30	20.0	20.0	60.0	100	5
Total	77.1	16.7	6.2	100	11,929	77.5	16.4	6.1	100	9,110	75.9	17.5	6.7	100	2,820

Source Author's calculations based on data from GLSS 2005/06

The data analysis above confirms the views expressed by the Minister of Education. Specifically, the issue of distance was referred to as a constraining factor to school access by the Minister, who mentioned that:

> [...] the effort to send the children to school would also be dependent upon the location of the school, the nearest school, where the child should attend. Now, if it is remote, and a young child of 5 or 6 should traverse that distance in order to get to school, some parents may not be too happy about this situation and they will wish they had the school very close to them. [...] Efforts are being made by the central government, in collaboration with the local government, to ensure [...] [the] building of more schools—so that the school will not be more than 3 or 4 kilometres from the community to enable the children to feel safe and secure in accessing the school.

According to the Ministry of Local Government and Rural Development (2006), policy dictates that a primary school must be within 5 km of a locality, while taking its population density into account. Nearly all of the government's resources allocated to the education sector over the past years, however, are for teacher salaries (96 % in 2009), while only 0.1 % is earmarked for investment needed for instance to build and rehabilitate schools based on EMIS expenditure data. Over the period 2001/02–2009/10, EMIS data indicate that about 3,300 new primary schools were built in the country largely with the aim of reducing travel time to school for children, increasing from 15,285 to 18,579 school structures nationwide, which are generally funded externally. Given that calculations here indicate that the average growth rate of school constructions was 2.4 % per year during this period, this suggests that it did not surpass the pace of natural growth since the basic school-age population has increased at an estimated 2.7 % annually since 2000. Widened access coupled with population growth has led to schools in many communities being increasingly overcrowded, with the number of pupils per primary school rising from 169.2 to 207.5 between 2001/02 and 2008/09 based on calculations of EMIS data.

Finally, this analysis argues that a supply-driven strategy of constructing more school facilities—at least in the medium and long-term—is likely to slowly reach its limits in attracting out-of-school children and especially keeping them in the system, for whom mainly demand-side policies will be most effective. In the short-term, however, sustained intervention to construct more schools is still needed.

Urbanisation and Population Density

Ghana became an urban society in 2008. Over half of the population since then resides in urban areas, with urban being defined by the Government of Ghana (2006) as a community with 5,000 persons or more. A poverty and migration assessment by the World Bank (2010d) identified urbanisation over the period 1992–2006 to be a phenomenon restricted to the South, where most cities are located, whereas the urbanisation rate in the North indeed fell from 19 to 16 % during this period.

Education density is linked to population density partly due to the provision of educational services at more affordable costs. A central explanation for the spatial relationship between population density and school attendance is that it is typically the most politically and financially difficult to build school infrastructure, deliver basic educational services including deploying teachers and increase demand for schooling (due to high opportunity costs) in areas where living settlements tend to be small and sparsely populated. Where people live dispersed over large areas such as in the Northern region (5.5 primary-age children and 2.1 lower secondary-age children per sq. km), there tends to be poor access to roads but also electricity and other amenities, bringing challenges and higher costs to educational organisation and management. In the North, the nature of many community settlements is such that it is not rare to find them consisting of about 10 households which can be widely scattered (see also Akyeampong 2004). This is where serving the educational needs and rights of children and youth face severe implementation constraints. In contrast, it is estimated that an average of 173.8 primary-age children live within a square kilometre in the Greater Accra region and 86.6 children of lower secondary-age in 2010 (calculations using Ghana Statistical Service and EMIS data).

Multifactor Educational Deprivation by Geographic Location

The share of children 6–14 years old who do not attend school is three times larger in the North than the South. Table 4.4 examines the spatial profile of children across different areas of the country who are currently outside the school system. It merges geographic variables and school non-attendance rates with data on household welfare levels, sex, age and other geographic metrics. The results here may have greater policy relevance compared to those for older population groups, given that education policy instruments can more easily impact the 6–14-year-old population relative to older adolescents and especially adults, who are much more likely to be active in the labour force.

Several interesting findings emerge from the data analysis. The differences among in and out-of-school children are large, especially in Northern Ghana. One of the most vulnerable groups are rural Northerners, as about one-third of children falling into this group do not participate in school—30.3 % of 6–14-year olds and 35.6 % of 6–7-year olds. The 6–7-year-old cohort consistently suffers from greater educational exclusion and deprivation than older basic school-age children. Furthermore, the urban poor, although constituting a relatively small share of the 6–14-year-old population in society at 3.2 %, are a very disadvantaged group, even compared to their rural poor counterparts. From a perspective of the most marginalised, data indicate that the likelihood that girls 6–14 years old from the poorest quintile who live in the rural countryside of the Northern region are attending school is the same as the likelihood that they are excluded from the school system (50 %).

Table 4.4 Share of children aged 6–14 who did not attend school in the academic year 2008/09, by geographic indicators and (dis-)advantaged groups

All shares refer to school non-attendance rates out of 100 %	Total	North	South	Rural	Urban	Poorest quintile	Richest quintile	Girl	Boy	Total observations
Total	15.6	28.4	9.3	18.9	9.6	29.4	7.4	15.2	15.9	11,589
North	28.4	–	–	30.3	20.0	33.8	12.1	27.5	29.1	3,820
South	9.3	–	–	10.8	7.4	18.1	6.9	9.7	8.9	7,769
Rural	18.9	30.3	10.8	–	–	29.1	3.1	18.0	19.6	7,485
Urban	9.6	20.0	7.4	–	–	36.9	8.0	10.6	8.6	4,104
Western region	11.9	–	–	14.3	7.8	20.2	10.1	12.7	11.1	1,036
Central region	14.2	–	–	12.9	16.7	25.8	20.9	13.8	14.6	911
Greater Accra region	8.8	–	–	11.4	8.3	36.4	7.6	12.1	5.4	1,100
Volta region	10.9	–	–	11.2	10.2	21.4	3.2	8.5	13.3	980
Eastern region	10.9	–	–	12.2	8.3	18.8	6.6	12.2	9.6	1,127
Ashanti region	3.6	–	–	3.7	3.4	10.1	1.7	4.1	3.0	1,571
Brong Ahafo region	8.4	–	–	11.3	3.4	15.4	0.0	7.4	9.5	1,044
Northern region	40.5	–	–	42.8	33.0	47.6	22.0	42.6	38.6	1,528
Upper East region	17.9	–	–	19.6	6.2	21.6	5.0	14.0	21.3	1,065
Upper West region	22.3	–	–	25.8	6.1	28.3	7.9	20.6	23.8	1,227
Capital, large city	8.9	20.1	7.6	–	–	26.7	7.1	10.4	7.3	1,585
Small city	7.1	10.7	5.8	–	–	14.8	7.2	6.8	7.4	1,558
Town	12.4	28.5	8.4	–	–	34.6	9.8	12.5	12.3	2,644
Countryside	21.2	31.3	12.1	–	–	29.2	0.0	20.5	21.7	5,802

Source Author's calculations based on data from GDHS

Note Place of residence for a large or small city, town or countryside is established by the survey interviewer's observation (GDHS 2009). Data on attendance for 6–7-year olds by quintile levels within regions should be read with caution as there are fewer than 30 observations for several regions

The fact that cross-regional differences among educationally deprived children are very large, with 40.5 % of the 6–14-year-old cohort not attending school in the Northern region compared to 3.6 % in the Ashanti region, has direct policy implications. These large disparities provide evidence that there is a need to rethink the scope of current nation-wide policies such as the capitation grant aimed at widening access (discussed in detail in Chap. 8) and that the geographic targeting of particular regions—especially the three Northern regions—is likely to be the most viable and cost-effective approach to speed up educational convergence between lagging and leading regions.

Conclusion and Policy Implications: The Geographic Isolation of the North

Birth place is one of the strongest predictors of an individual's future human capital in Ghana. The North, where rurality and low population density come together, is the most geographically disadvantaged area in the country and the geographic divide between the North and South has been identified as one of the most important external influences shaping the educational landscape in Ghana. If the seven Southern regions in the country constituted their own country, nearly every 17-year-old would have already attained primary completion (96.8 %), while if the three Northern regions formed their own country, almost one quarter of youth of this age (23 %) would not have had this opportunity (based on 2008/09 GDHS data analysis). Findings here indicate that possibly the central obstacle for the country to attain the second MDG is how it will be able to open access and ensure transition for all children living in the North, home to the vast majority of the chronically underserved at all levels of education. Causes of the North–South educational divide revolve around (i) the past political neglect of and current limited political attention on the North reflected by inadequately targeted policy arrangements, (ii) stark geographic isolation, low population density and distances to schools in some areas, (iii) greater school resource deficiency at all levels not only related to funding but also personnel (lower shares of teachers) and infrastructure (fewer school facilities) as shown above and (iv) the lower demand for schooling which is closely linked to the negligible rates of return to primary education in this part of the country, as the vast majority of Northern households have agricultural livelihoods (and as shown in Chap. 6 there are no income gains for even basic school completers who later work in self-employed agriculture).

Education remains spatially very uneven and therefore policy needs to accommodate this. Ghanaians expect and hope for more rapid education development and convergence in access and attainment at all levels, the latter of which is likely to take more than several decades even in the presence of targeted interventions. Besides the economic arguments in favour of tapping the North's potential, it may be politically unsustainable to allow coming generations of Northerners to remain straggling behind. If public service delivery is not expanded for Northerners, achieving social cohesion and equity in the country will not be possible. The situation must be taken seriously as this has been since 2002 a major cause of the political and economic division of neighbouring, conflict-ridden Cote d'Ivoire that continues today. Because the educationally-impoverished of Ghana are highly concentrated in the North where for example, only 19 % of the total primary-age population lives, there are strong arguments in favour of geographic targeting towards Northern Ghana of some already existing nationwide education interventions in order to promote greater North–South connectivity and create a regional balance. To sustainably push regional convergence in education forward, a policy of at least equal access for the North, if not also more equitable outcomes, will be necessary. The richer South, which would not be targeted but is likely to carry a larger financial burden of the programmes targeting the North via tax collection, could potentially pose some political difficulties in terms of implementation (Chap. 8 covers an in-depth policy discussion). In closing, a central implication from the analysis is that any strategy to alleviate education poverty and exclusion in Ghana that does not place the North at the forefront is likely deemed to fail, while part of the content in subsequent chapters is to recognise the particular determinants of educational exclusion at the individual, household and community level.

Chapter 5
Health Status of Children: Vulnerability and Educational Effects

Good health is essential for an individual's educational progression. The Government of Ghana underpinned this fact in its Education Strategic Plan 2003–2015, making the promotion of good health and sanitation in schools and the delivery of HIV/AIDS prevention programmes two of the ten main policy goals at the basic school level (Ministry of Education 2009). Still, about 5 % of households in 2003 reported illness as the reason why their child was not enrolled in primary or lower secondary school based on data collected from the Core Welfare Indicators Questionnaire Survey (GSS 2003), while this specific question is not captured in more recent surveys.

This chapter sheds light on the complex interactions between education, health and life skills, with particular attention given to constraints of Ghanaians' health status on their education and vice versa. These interactions are analysed for five issues of particular relevance for the Ghanaian education context: fertility, malnutrition, malaria, HIV/AIDS and water and sanitation. Further, regression analysis and a cost-benefit incidence are conducted to assess the impact of education and the efficiency of education spending on social and health behaviours, evaluating how and to what extent different levels of completed education impact key health indicators (fertility, pregnancy, natal care etc.) and the lives of Ghanaians. Finally, it examines the degree to which cross-sectoral improvements such as those across the education MDG and the respective health-related MDGs (1, 5, 6 and 7) are mutually reinforcing.

The Complementary Nature of Health Status and Schooling

School-age children are a vulnerable group due to a number of health hazards. Data analysis in the following shows that children's health status helps to influence when and if they begin school, how they function in school and the duration they remain in school. Table 5.1 crosses health and education data to see if and to what extent differences exist in health indicators between in- and out-of-school children, and matches the respective data for their age, geographic location, household wealth and sex. It provides valuable insight and sheds light on the interlocking health-related factors that affect school participation and illustrates that the differences among these two groups

A. Krauss, *External Influences and the Educational Landscape*,
SpringerBriefs in Economics, DOI: 10.1007/978-1-4614-4936-2_5,

Table 5.1 Share of children aged 6–14 who did not attend school in the academic year 2008/09, by health indicators and (dis-advantaged groups)

All shares refer to school non-attendance rates out of 100 %	Total	North	South	Rural	Urban	Poorest quintile	Richest quintile	Girl	Boy	Total obs.
Total	15.6	28.4	9.3	18.9	9.6	29.4	7.4	15.2	15.9	11,593
Unimproved drinking water source: river/dam/lake/ponds/stream/canal/irrigation	22.7	49.6	13.8	23.5	14.5	32.3	0.0	22.5	22.9	1,484
Improved drinking water source: public tap/standpipe	11.8	26.4	8.3	14.6	8.7	41.3	6.0	11.0	10.7	2,866
Unimproved toilet: no facility/bush/field	27.1	30.6	14.7	28.0	19.7	31.9	18.8	26.2	27.8	3,822
Improved toilet: ventilated improved pit latrine	9.4	19.2	7.7	10.0	9.0	27.7	6.9	9.6	9.2	3,805
Food cooked in the house using an open fire	26.0	36.9	7.9	27.0	20.6	38.8	6.5	25.9	26.1	2,932
Slept under a mosquito net the night before the survey	14.1	22.8	9.8	16.4	7.3	24.1	6.2	13.1	15.1	1,372
Had received any messages in past year telling you to seek treatment for fever	13.8	25.2	8.5	16.7	8.7	26.7	6.7	13.5	14.1	8,908
Had received any messages in past year telling you to complete full course of malaria drugs	13.7	23.4	8.6	16.4	9.3	25.8	8.2	13.5	13.8	6,965
Time to get to water source, less than 30 min	13.8	26.7	9.2	16.8	9.1	27.4	7.4	13.6	14.0	9,977
Time to get to water source, more than 30 min	26.6	31.9	11.2	28.1	17.1	34.0	8.3	25.8	27.3	1,572

Source Author's calculations based on data from GDHS

are large and particularly large in Northern Ghana and in the bottom welfare quintile. Disaggregating the data by gender indicates that girls are not a disadvantaged group, and in fact have overall slightly higher school attendance rates compared to boys.

Sanitation and health conditions appear at times to play a larger role than welfare levels in influencing school participation. Children from the richest quintile who use a bush or field as a toilet (although a very small share of this population) have a lower attendance rate at 81.2 % than the average Ghanaian child at 84.4 %, which implies that the type of toilet facility used has the potential—given its health externalities—to predict attendance better than quintile levels. In later sections of this chapter the underlying causes and explanations of such correlations are discussed in detail.

School-age children who slept under a mosquito net the night before the survey (which likely implies that they generally sleep under one) have only slightly higher attendance rates at 85.9 % compared to those who did not at 84.2 %. This suggests that, under the assumption that a mosquito net is used properly, malaria prevention behaviour such as mosquito net use does not strongly influence school absence or attendance in the country as a whole. However, children in the North who slept under a mosquito net increased their likelihood of attending school by 6.3 % (from 70.9 to 77.2 %).

Health-related issues are strong influencers of a child's age at initial enrolment. Data shows that larger differences exist between in- and out-of-school children aged 6–7 compared to older basic school-age children and much larger differences when disaggregated by location or welfare level. 21.2 % of 6–7 year old children (24.1 % of 6 year olds) have not yet attended a school. For instance, 6–7 year old children, who use a river, pond or similar source for their drinking water, have on average lower school attendance rates whether living in the South of the country at 75.6 % or in the North at 46.4 % compared to the average Ghanaian child of this age with any water source at 78.8 %. This implies that a poor quality water source, given its health implications on children, can potentially play a larger role than residency in either the North or the South in helping to determine school attendance.

Fertility Rates

Ghana is experiencing not only considerable educational and economic change but also changes in regards to reproductive behaviour patterns, particularly reduced fertility. The latter will contribute to reduced strain on persistent school enrolment influxes and likely to higher standards of living for Ghanaians. Calculations of GDHS data reveal that the total fertility rate has strongly declined over the past two decades, from 6.4 children per woman in 1988 to 4.0 children per woman in 2008. How much of this fertility transition can be attributed to increased levels of education? Later in this chapter a regression analysis is conducted finding that increased educational attainment explains the majority of the differences in fertility levels in Ghana. If girls complete the compulsory basic cycle, they have on average one less child later in life, while the completion of university education explains a reduction of almost two childbirths per woman, with other influences held constant such as age, locality, occupation/wealth and physical access to a

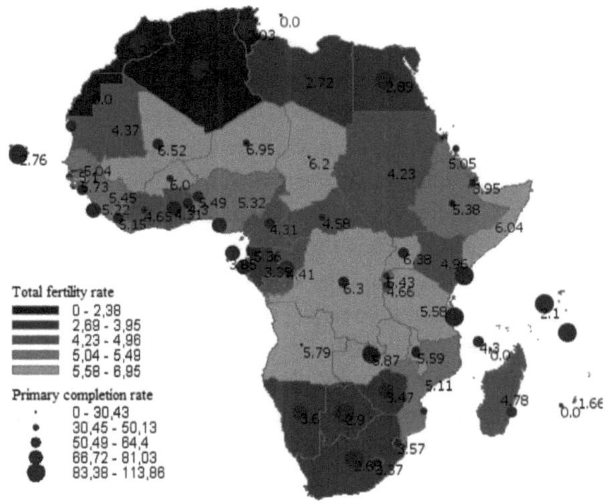

Map 5.1 Comparison of fertility rates and primary completion rates across Africa, 2008 or latest year
Source Author's illustration based on data from Africa Development Indicators
Note Data is not available for Western Sahara. Data for primary completion rates reflect the latest year between 2001 and 2008 and for total fertility rates between 2006 and 2008

health facility. The results suggest that, although this shift in reproductive behaviour is largely explained by the improved educational profile among women of reproductive age, other determinants of reduced fertility are urban locality and women's reproductive history (reduced infant and child mortality that decreases women's childbearing desires).

A spatial picture provided in Map 5.1 of the average number of children women give birth to across Africa provides a measure of which countries tend to (1) have stronger pronatalist attitudes, (2) face more difficulties in terms of educational funding and capacity to ensure all children are sent to school and (3) will continue placing pressure on (in many cases) already overstretched education systems in years to come. Crossing data presented in Map 5.1 on the fertility levels of 15–49-year-old mothers with primary completion rates reveals that none of the 10 African countries with a total fertility rate below three has a primary completion rate below 83 %, while none of the seven African countries with a total fertility rate of six or above has a primary completion rate above 55 %. The multi-factoral relationship of geographic remoteness, lower educational capital and higher fertility, which are widely regarded as key components of a poverty trap, is most pervasive and persistent in some of the landlocked Sahel countries and Central African countries.

Education and fertility have interlocking synergies. Ghanaian women aged 15–49 who have no education give birth to an average of 4.6 children compared to 3 children among those with primary schooling and 2.4 children if they have tertiary education. In addition, all mothers aged 15–49 with 10 or more living children have either no schooling or only incomplete primary schooling, and no mothers with more than 6 children have any higher education, suggesting that women who are more educationally disadvantaged are more likely to give birth to more children (based on 2008/09 GDHS data). In a circular relationship, a mother's level of fertility is subsequently a good predictor of the prospects of how far her children can move up the educational ladder, with educational status later in life being influenced in good measure by the number of siblings one has competing over limited household resources, given that 53.6 % of Ghanaians live on less than $2 (PPP) per day (World Development data for 2008)—an issue discussed in detail in Chap. 7. Furthermore, data from the Core Welfare Indicators Questionnaire Survey indicate that about 2 % of households reported pregnancy or childbearing as the reason why their child was not enrolled in lower secondary school (GSS 2003).

What explains education's impact on fertility? The duration of schooling especially for females inversely affects childbearing desires, as being more educated can:

- Build job skills to enter the labour force later, which helps to promote postponed marriage;
- Enhance financial independence (shown in Chap. 6 covering income), whereas the less educated often regard having more children as a form of social security, as field research indicates;
- Increase the opportunity costs related to childbearing, as adolescent females receiving higher levels of education are more likely to avoid interrupting school plans, while a study of rural Ghana by Fentiman et al. (1999) found that pregnant students are often compelled to drop out, since some head teachers do not permit adolescent females to come back to school after childbirth and stated that it discourages early pregnancy among peers;
- Help to provide females with greater levels of literacy and better means to inform and articulate themselves such that they tend to have greater capacity to make decisions at home and influence family planning issues; and,
- Mean greater exposure to instructional content on sexual reproductive health, which field research conducted for this analysis in 2010 with primary students interviewed in the capital Accra indicates begins to be mediated typically in the 2nd or 3rd year and already instils children with knowledge on contraceptive use.

On the one hand, although almost all Ghanaians have some knowledge of contraceptive methods, especially those who are well educated, this does not appear to translate inevitably into behavioural changes, given that only 13.6 % of married women without any schooling use some form of contraception while 30.4 % of those who have upper secondary or beyond do. On the other hand, among youth who are sexually active, sex education appears effective in promoting safer sex practices, with only 5.2 % of young women aged 15–24 without schooling using a condom the first time they had sex compared to 26 % of

Table 5.2 One's level of education by information acquisition and sexual behaviour modification, 2008/09

	Input: Information acquisition				Output: Contraceptive/intercourse/fertility behaviour modification				
	Knowledge of contraceptive methods: currently married who have heard of any modern method		No exposure to family planning messages by radio, television or newspaper		Married women's current use of any contraception method	15–24-year-old women who had sexual intercourse before age 15	18-24-year-old women who had sexual intercourse before age 18	15-24-year-old women who had sex and used a condom the 1st time	Ideal number of children for women
	Women	Men	Women	Men					
No education	93.7	97.9	49.2	37.5	13.6	11.0	55.0	5.2	5.8
Primary	99.5	99.4	40.8	36.6	26.6	13.9	61.9	19.5	4.3
Lower sec.	99.4	100	26.9	23.3	27.4	7.3	48.9	26.0	3.9
Upper sec.+	100	100	12.3	13.1	30.4	1.7	19.8	41.5	3.4
Total	97.8	99.5	31.9	24.2	23.5	7.8	43.9	25.1	4.3
Number of obs.	2,876	1,950	4,916	4,058	2,876	1,902	1,298	1,159	4,831

Source Author's calculations based on GDHS data

Note All data, unless otherwise specified, reflects individuals 15–49 years of age. If more than one contraceptive method is used, only the most effective method is considered for 'married women's current use of contraception'

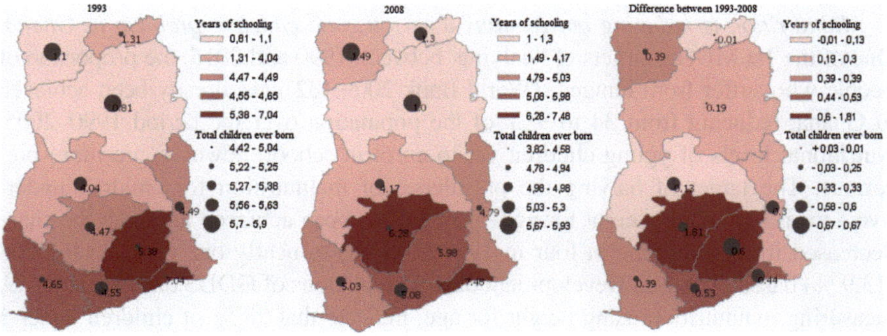

Map 5.2 Mothers' years of completed schooling and total number of children ever born, 1993 and 2008

Source Author's illustration based on GDHS data. *Note* The numbers indicated in the regions refer to years of schooling. Survey data calculations cover 13,298 women for 1993 and 11,841 women for 2008

those with completed primary and 41.5 % of those with at least upper secondary. The last column statistically illustrates that as women become more educated they have a stronger inclination to reduce their family size—by almost two children for those who complete the basic cycle. In sum, schooling can therefore be seen as a protection against early sexual activity, early pregnancy, HIV transmission and high childbearing desires (Table 5.2).

Mothers' years of schooling and levels of child births have largely stagnated in the North. Map 5.2 measures cross-regional differences in the years of schooling for mothers 15–49 years old and the number of children they have given birth to. Calculations of GDHS data, using the baseline year of 1993 together with 2008, reveal that over this period the number of years of completed schooling for mothers of this age who live in the South increased on average by 0.6 years compared to 0.2 in the North, while the number of total child births reduced by half a child (0.5) in the South and overall stagnated in the North (0.004) .

Malnutrition

In the first years of life, children have similar growth potential, but inequitable opportunities in basic schooling can limit a child's cognitive growth while nutritional deficiencies can limit a child both physically and cognitively. Compounding this situation, many young malnourished children are out of school. This section analyses the nutrition-schooling relationship and, in particular, it examines to what extent infant and child nutrition helps to influence the age at which a child enrols in school and how differences in school participation patterns are shaped by differences in children's and youth's nutritional status.

Malnutrition is reducing but remains a serious and endemic problem in Ghana. One of the 1st MDG's targets of "halving, between 1990 and 2015, the proportion of people who suffer from hunger" (World Bank 2009:132) has already been achieved in Ghana, reducing from 34 to 9 % of the population over the period 1990–2005. Nutritional levels of young children yet to enrol in school, however, are more precarious. The target of halving the prevalence of malnutrition for children under-five—measured using weight for age—has not yet been achieved although the share decreased from about one in four in 1990 (24.1 %) to nearly one in seven in 2008 (13.9 %) based on Africa Development data. Calculations of GDHS data for 2008/09, measuring malnutrition using height for age, indicate that 28 % of children under-5 is chronically undernourished and short/stunted for their given age and 9.8 % of children of this age group are severely stunted. Although not at all a reflection of malnutrition, about one in three teachers (36 %) reported sometimes coming to school hungry, as a teacher questionnaire in Ghana reveals (Ministry of Education 2010).

High individual, educational and social costs are linked to widespread malnutrition. At the individual level, the large shares of child malnutrition in the country mean that many children are not only subject to irreversible physical and mental stunting, but are also more susceptible to infections and delayed recovery from sickness, while they may also have decreased energy and motivation levels. From an educational perspective, the large shares of child malnutrition are a major factor that impinges on the sector, helping to affect late enrolment, attendance patterns and early dropout, as this section highlights. Malnutrition can also limit students' attention span, constrain their cognitive capacity to retain information and adversely influence their school performance. In terms of social effects, the large shares of child malnutrition drive the incidence of child mortality in the country, with undernourishment being an underlying cause of about half of all child deaths (World Bank 2009).

To what extent do malnourished/anaemic children enrol later in school? Analysis of GDHS data for 2008/09 indicates that an alarming 72.3 % of pre-primary school-age children (4–5-year olds) are classified as being anaemic—either mildly, moderately or severely (based on WHO criteria)—which is mainly caused by insufficient iron intake and can lead to impaired mental and physical development and, in extreme cases, even mortality (GDHS 2009). A study in the Eastern region of Ghana by Fentiman et al. (2001) found similar results, with 70 % of all primary-age children suffering from anaemia. School attendance rates of 4–5-year olds are crossed here (as GDHS does not collect data on nutrition for 6–14-year olds) with their respective levels of anaemia, which data indicate is very highly correlated to other indicators of malnutrition such as height-for-age or weight-for-age. Results indicate that nearly half of the children (49 %) falling into this age group are either moderately or severely anaemic, while over one quarter of these children (27.7 %) are not anaemic (the remaining 23.3 % are mildly anaemic). 64.4 % of children in this age group who are non-anaemic attended school during the academic year 2008/09 while this share drops to 50.8 % for those who suffer from moderate or severe anaemia, which accounts for the largest group in the 4–5-year-old population. The findings provide data-driven evidence that children's nutritional status—measured by levels of anaemia—may help to explain their school participation since the likelihood to attend school for children of this age group, who live in the wealthiest and most urban region (the Greater Accra region), reduces by 13.6 % if they suffer from moderate or severe anaemia and by 7.4 % for those living in the poorest and most rural region (the Northern region).

A study of rural Ghana by Fentiman et al. (1999) found that among parents who were questioned why a child of official school-age had not attended school, some responded that their child was too 'small' or 'young'. In spite of the appropriate age of enrolment into kindergarten being four and into primary being six, it is likely that some parents with malnourished children delay enrolment as a result of their children not yet being mature enough or mentally not developed enough. A study conducted in small rural villages of Ghana found that parents' assessment of their children's readiness for school is generally unrelated to age in part due to most parents in these areas not keeping close track of their children's age (Awedoba et al. 2003). Some parents may therefore use height or another proxy rather than actual age to determine at what point their children are ready for school. Field research conducted for this analysis in 2010 indicates that if children are physically too weak and small to perform specific tasks assigned by parents, especially relevant among agrarian households, then parents may delay their school enrolment. Also, some parents may believe that their children must be 'older' (bigger) to walk longer distances to school.

Primary one students are less anaemic than those out of school but reflect a wide age range. Figure 5.1 provides evidence of the disparities in anaemia levels between those attending primary one and those outside of the school system—bearing in mind (as mentioned) that GDHS does not collect data on nutrition for

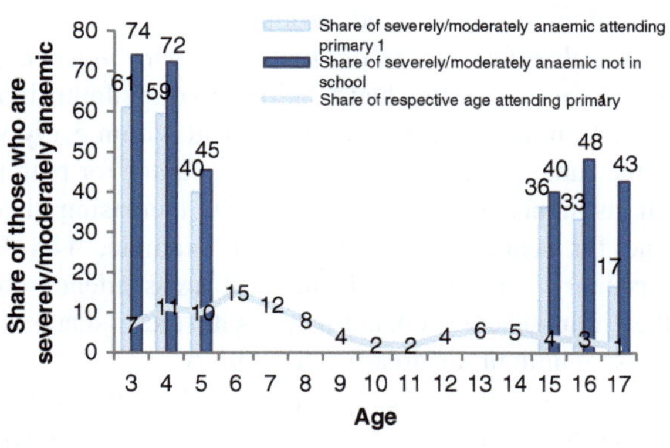

Fig. 5.1 Age range of primary one students, and the share of those in primary one and out of school who are severely/moderately anaemic by age, 2008/09
Source Author's illustration based on calculations of GDHS data
Note The survey sample of the group attending primary one covers 3,730 individuals. GDHS (2009) classifications of the severity of anaemia are based on WHO criteria and distinguish between three groups relative to haemoglobin levels in individuals' blood: mild anaemia (10.0–10.9 g/dL), moderate anaemia (7.0–9.9 g/dL) and severe anaemia (less than 7.0 g/dL)

6–14-year olds. It indicates that anaemic children and youth are consistently more vulnerable to not attend primary one and that younger children are most strongly affected by anaemia. Three findings are particularly alarming. First of all, the age of children and youth at the point of initial enrolment reflects a broad age range in Ghana, varying from 3 to 24 years of age in class one of primary (although the share of youth 18 or above accounts for only 4.8 % of the total). Second, 85 % of children and youth attending primary one are not the official age of six, although 55.4 % are between 3 and 7 years of age. Third, almost one in every three (30.3 %) who attend primary one are 11 years of age or older, and overage children in school are much more likely to not finish the primary cycle but rather leave school prematurely to begin working without even a basic set of skills and competencies acquired in school, as illustrated in Chap. 6.

One of the most critical policy needs in the sector is to ensure enrolment at the proper age. It is possible to classify the 15.6 % of out-of-school children 6–14 years of age in 2008/09 (GDHS data) into three categories, for which data analysis here reveals that 33.3 % of this sub-group have attended but eventually dropped out while about 28.5 % are likely to enter late and about 38.2 % are never expected to attend. All three of these sub-groups are educationally either very vulnerable or deprived. About one in every four children 6 years of age (24.1 %) did not attend school in the academic year 2008/09 and one in five (19.8 %) have never been to school based on GDHS calculations. By initially beginning school late, a waste of educational endowment is combined with a loss of greater household income given that when children become older, the value of their time rises. With higher opportunity costs for older children to attend school (discussed in Chap. 6), field research indicates that late enrolment is known to often translate into early drop out and thus early integration into a less-skilled labour force. From a public finance perspective, the high levels of being over-age in school in Ghana also induce increased public costs for education due to higher repetition rates.

Anaemia consistently influences school non-attendance independent of location or welfare. Table 5.3 shows that the dual relationship of malnutrition (measured by being anaemic) and non-attendance is widely spread within every wealth quintile level and within the same geographic areas of the country for both pre-school-age children as well as upper secondary age youth, increasing thereby anemia's explanatory value for school participation. For example, 44.4 % of anaemic children of pre-primary age who reside in rural areas attend school compared to 52.2 % of their non-anaemic counterparts, with these shares being 73.0 and 77.4 % among those within urban areas of the country.

Participatory field research conducted in late 2010 for this analysis in Accra provides further nuanced evidence and indicates that primary students interviewed went to sleep hungry on average several times a week, and are hungry at school about two to three out of five school days a week although they reported that this does not always affect concentration in class. Conversely, there was overall no significant problem of going to bed hungry or being hungry during school among senior high students interviewed. Another interesting finding is that some of the primary students questioned indicated that meat eaten at home is usually always

Table 5.3 School attendance rates of anaemic versus non-anaemic children of pre-primary age and youth of upper secondary age, for the academic year 2008/09

	School attendance rates of pre-primary children (aged 4–5) who are:				School attendance rates of upper secondary youth (aged 15–17)[a] who are:			
	Anaemic	Non-anaemic	Total	Number of obs.	Anaemic	Non-anaemic	Total	Number of obs.
Total	51.4	64.4	55.0	627	65.5	73.2	68.3	590
Location								
Rural	44.4	52.2	46.1	432	67.1	75.2	70.0	340
Urban	73.0	77.4	74.9	195	63.3	70.7	66.0	250
North	41.0	42.0	41.3	223	57.5	71.0	63.5	156
South	57.9	73.4	62.6	404	67.9	74.3	70.1	434
Wealth quintile								
Lowest	35.5	37.2	35.8	215	56.2	68.4	61.5	130
Second	50.0	55.2	51.1	141	66.3	71.8	68.1	119
Middle	51.6	67.9	56.5	92	71.0	81.6	74.8	107
Fourth	74.1	75.0	74.5	94	67.9	78.4	71.1	121
Highest	84.3	91.2	87.1	85	66.2	69.1	67.3	113
Mother's education								
No schooling	39.9	32.6	38.5	239	–	–	–	–
Primary	54.7	70.6	58.9	129	–	–	–	–
Lower secondary	65.5	73.9	68.4	133	–	–	–	–
Upper secondary+	75.0	88.9	81.0	42	–	–	–	–

Source Author's calculations based on GDHS data

Note [a] Given that GDHS only collects data on anaemia for 0–5 year olds (both boys and girls) and for women 15–49 years of age, data for upper secondary age youth in the table only refer to females. Children and youth are classified here as being anaemic whether mildly, moderately or severely. GDHS data limitations do not allow for mothers' level of education to be matched with attendance rates among upper secondary age youth

reserved for older household members, which contributes to explaining why the vast majority of children are iron deficient.

Schooling seems to generate an intergenerational effect on good nutrition. Table 5.4 crosses GDHS data on mothers' level of education with pre-specified indicators that measure malnutrition levels for children under-5 using their standard deviation from the median of the international growth standards set by the World Health Organisation (for methodology see GDHS 2009). It shows that 29.6 % of children under-5, who have mothers without schooling, are chronically undernourished and short/stunted for their given age (below minus two standard deviations [−2 SD]). Furthermore, more than one in every ten children under-5 (11.8 %), whose mothers have no education, are severely stunted (below minus three standard deviations [−3 SD]). These corresponding figures for mothers with upper secondary schooling or beyond are about half—17.5 and 5.3 %, respectively. One explanation is likely that more educated mothers tend to give greater significance to their children's nutrition and health and inform themselves more often about their own nutritional needs and those of their children.

School feeding programme: a big challenge is the unequal distribution of schools. The school feeding programme is a policy instrument used by the

Table 5.4 Nutritional status of children under five by their mothers' level of schooling, 2008/09

Mothers' level of education	Height-for-age			Weight-for-height				Weight-for-age				Number of children
	% below –3 SD	% below –2 SD	Mean Z-score (SD)	% below –3 SD	% below –2 SD	% above +2 SD	Mean Z-score (SD)	% below –3 SD	% below –2 SD	% above +2 SD	Mean Z-score (SD)	
No education	11.8	29.6	−1.2	3.5	11.4	4.6	−0.4	3.7	17.2	1.5	−1	738
Primary	10.4	31.6	−1.2	2.1	7.7	4.8	−0.2	3.4	13.5	2	−0.8	545
Lower sec.	7.4	25.1	−1	1.7	8.3	5.5	−0.2	2.8	12.4	2.2	−0.7	783
Upper sec.+	5.3	17.5	−0.6	1.1	5.4	7.9	0.1	0.6	6.8	3.3	−0.3	218
Total	9.8	28	−1.1	2.2	8.5	5.3	−0.2	3.1	13.9	1.9	−0.8	2,525

Source Calculations based on GDHS data

Note Height-for-age is an anthropometric indicator used to gauge chronic, long-term nutritional deficiency, while weight-for-height measures a child's body mass relative to his or her body height and illustrates present nutritional status that can reflect acute, short-term inadequate dietary intake. Weight-for-age uses both of these measurements as a composite index, incorporating acute and chronic undernourishment (GDHS 2009) government (1) to offer a social safety net for children of impoverished households and reduce malnutrition rates, (2) to incentivise poor parents to ensure their children are enrolled by reducing indirect costs of attending school and therefore (3) to help make youth more productive later in life. An indirect transfer to households (i.e. to schools) of the value of food directly relieves expenses especially for poor families, as calculations of GLSS data for 2005/06 reveal that food expenses constitute by far the largest share of household expenditure for schooling (at about 45 % of a student's expenses for public school and 29 % for private school).

First piloted in ten schools in Ghana in late 2005, the school feeding programme reached 1,040,000 pupils in beneficiary kindergarten and primary schools by late 2010 (World Bank 2010e). It is important to mention that out-of-school children are, by definition, not recipients of the free school meal scheme. 20.7 % of children in primary school were beneficiaries in 2008/09 (EMIS data). An inventory of the implementation of the school feeding programme conducted in all regions by the Netherlands Development Organisation (2008) found that only about half of the beneficiary schools (50.6 %) served meals every day during the academic year 2007/08. From the school's perspective, some explained that these low compliance levels are a consequence of late and inadequate release of funds which are to total 30 pesewas daily per child (US$0.28 at 2008 exchange rates).

The supply of the school feeding programme does not reflect the demand. Evidence is provided throughout this analysis that data does not always guide policy. In the case of the school feeding programme, its current target schools are indeed determined by data although for a variety of indirect and non-nutrition related indicators such as levels of access to roads, water and electricity, conflict or flood vulnerable areas and school infrastructure (World Bank 2010d). Improving the programme's geographic targeting to food insecure and poor areas would yield much more positive effects for the North. A simple needs assessment of the school feeding programme using GDHS data for 2008/09 can highlight the regions with the greatest share of people living in the poorest quintile and with the greatest share of severely malnourished children under five, measured as being severely stunted using height-for-age. It is children under five whose physical and mental development would gain most from improved nutrition, while the school feeding programme also targets pre-primary pupils (4–5 year olds). Figure 5.2 points to very poor targeting of the programme, and provides data-driven evidence, once again, of the North's political discrimination. 23.1 % of pupils are beneficiaries of the school feeding programme in the South, although only 4.2 % live in the poorest quintile and 9 % of children under-5 are severely stunted/malnourished here. Conversely, in the North, where 23.5 % live in the poorest quintile and 12.4% of children under-5 are severely stunted/malnourished, the share of pupil recipients is about two times lower at only 12.4 % in spite of the high demand in this part of the country. This offers proof of the very poor allocation of the total GH¢32 million (US$30.6 million at 2008 exchange rates) disbursed for the programme in 2008 (government data for annual budget). One political economy consideration is that the clientelistic nature of Ghanaian politics could help to explain why the Ashanti region (with one of the lowest needs) is proportionately the largest recipient of the programme since the

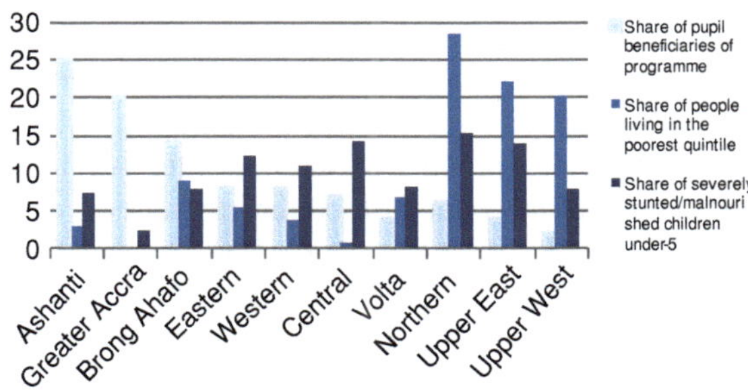

Fig. 5.2 Needs assessment versus policy targeting of the school feeding programme for the academic year 2008/09
Source Author's illustration based on calculations of data from GDHS 2008/09 (welfare and nutrition), and the Annual Operating Plan, Government of Ghana 2009 (school feeding beneficiaries)

region is the bastion of the ruling party that created the programme. The findings here of the programme's severe misallocation are consistent with previous research indicating that in 2006 only 13.1 % of school lunch beneficiaries came from the bottom quintile while 25.8 % came from the top quintile (World Bank 2010e).

In sum, given that it is not possible to retrieve severe nutritional deficiencies, stunting, enrolling late and being overage in school, universal primary completion (likely even access to primary one) may appear statistically unattainable in light of the high levels of malnutrition and anaemia in the country.

Malaria

Malaria is the most common infectious disease facing Ghanaians and the most common cause of death in the country, with malnutrition being an underlying cause of many of these deaths especially among children, due to weaker immune systems (World Bank 2009). The hardest hit region worldwide in terms of malaria prevalence is Africa, within which West Africa—and particularly Ghana—has some of the highest levels, as MARA (2004) mapping data illustrate. The number of malaria cases estimated for children under-5 in Ghana was 3.9 million out of a total under-5 population of 3.2 million children in 2006, implying that these children had on average more than one reported case of malaria within the year, while it is very likely that many cases of malaria are not reported (WHO 2010). Malaria, which is transmitted by a Anopheline mosquito bite (Dzator and Asafu-Adjaye 2004), is hyper-endemic in Ghana and represents 44 % of outpatient visits, 13 % of mortality in hospitals and 22 % of under-5 child deaths (De La Cruz et al. 2006).

4.5 % of school-age children suffer on a recurrent basis from malaria/fever, which entails educational costs due to fatigue and absenteeism. One of the targets of the 6th MDG is to "have halted by 2015 and begun to reverse the incidence of malaria" (World Bank 2009:133). Under the Education Strategic Plan 2010–2020—the main

Table 5.5 Mothers' educational status and the prevalence of fever among their children under-5 and anti-malarial treatment, 2008/09

	Children under-5 with fever, %	Of these children under-5 with fever, %			Number of obs.
		Visited a health facility or provider for advice or treatment	Took anti-malarial drugs	Took anti-malarial drugs same or next day	
No education	19.4	45.8	31.7	16.7	173
Primary	22.8	44.9	41.9	25.0	152
Lower secondary	18.4	55.4	49.9	25.1	169
Upper secondary+	19.9	69.6	61.5	39.3	50
Total	19.9	50.7	43.0	23.7	544

Source Calculations based on GDHS data

policy document of the Ministry of Education (2009)—the government acknowledges the "special significance" that the eradication of malaria would have on the education sector. According to the Ghana National Commission on Children (2000), about 16 % of school-age children experienced recurring health problems, among whom 28 % cited malaria/fever as the main reason, while fever is commonly used as a proxy for malaria in relevant tropical countries. Moreover, analysis of 2008/09 GDHS data indicates that children 6–14 years of age who slept under a mosquito net the night before the survey increased their likelihood of attending school by 1.7 % nationally and by 6.3 % in the North relative to those who did not.

Table 5.5 cross-tabulates data on mothers' levels of education with the prevalence of fever among their children under-five during the 2 weeks preceding the survey and with reported treatment rates. 69.6 % of mothers with at least upper secondary education sought advice or treatment for their child's fever from a health facility or provider compared to 45.8 % for those who have no education. Furthermore, children whose mothers have upper secondary schooling or beyond are twice as likely to take anti-malarial drugs when they have fever.

HIV/AIDS

HIV prevalence in Ghana was 1.9 % among the 15–49-year-old population in 2009, with estimates ranging from 1.7 to 2.2 % and projections indicating that the share will continue to increase (Ghana Health Service 2010). As the prevalence of HIV rises above about 1.7 %, according to UNAIDS (2010), the virus has the potential to become sustainable among the population. While Ghana has already surpassed this level, the prevalence remains below the 5 % threshold that characterises a generalised HIV/AIDS epidemic (Fobil and Soyiri 2006). In light of this and the fact that Ghana has one of the lowest HIV infection rates in sub-Saharan Africa, the country has a window of opportunity to control and reduce the spread of the disease. Yet, given that the national HIV prevalence rose in 2009 relative to 2008 levels and if it would raise to levels found in cities like Koforidua in the Eastern region at 5.8 % for the same year (Ghana Health Service 2010), the virus could increasingly shape the educational landscape creating more orphans and vulnerable groups of children. The number of children aged 0–14, who lost their mother or father or both parents to AIDS, is estimated to be about 140,500 in 2009—or 1.5 % of this age group. Many of whom face a large burden in life, not to mention their increased financial costs in terms of school expenditures. Moreover, about 25,700 children of basic school-age or younger (aged 0–14) live with HIV (Ghana Health Service 2010), suggesting that the prevalence of HIV for the respective child population is less than 1 %. The HIV prevalence among youth 15–24 years of age is estimated to be 1.3 % for females and 0.4 % for males (UNAIDS 2010). In terms of school instructors, a teacher questionnaire in Ghana reveals that 9 % of teachers believe that the impact of HIV/AIDS on teachers at their school has been serious (Ministry of Education 2010). Even if it is overall a small share of Ghanaians afflicted with HIV relative to other sub-Saharan countries, its potential spread remains a social threat which needs to be addressed.

Calculations of GDHS data show that 9.1 % of 6–14-year-old children have lost one or both parents, and among these orphans and vulnerable children 82.2 % attended school during the academic year 2008/09 compared to the national average of 84.4 % of children, illustrating near parity between these two groups of children. Findings may suggest that a certain degree of positive discrimination for these vulnerable children exists, towards which strong family and social ties (foster care) in Ghana contribute, as field research with primary students interviewed in 2010 indicates.

In a circular fashion, education can affect the spread of the virus. Only 1.6 % of men aged 15–49 without schooling, who had two or more partners in the past year, used a condom in comparison to 18.2 % for those with primary education and 41.9 % of men who have at least upper secondary schooling. A particularly important finding is that most youth 15–24 years of age have sexual intercourse and, for instance, only 5.2 % of females of this age without any schooling used a condom the first time they had sex compared to 26 % of those with completed primary and 41.5 % of those with at least upper secondary schooling. The implied finding is that—in the absence of effective sexual reproductive education in schools—HIV has the potential to spread rapidly, as the majority of youth are having sexual intercourse and do not always use condoms. This should be of policy concern because the population 24 years of age or younger accounts for 59.2 % of the total population (GDHS data calculations for 2008/09).

Water and Sanitation

One target of the 7th MDG is to "halve, by 2015, the proportion of people without sustainable access to safe drinking water and basic sanitation" (World Bank 2009:133). Improved access to potable water and sanitation is recognised in the government's Education Strategic Plan 2003–2015 as a fundamental precondition to attain the second MDG given that it reduces the frequency of child illness and absenteeism

(Government of Ghana 2003). In the revised Education Strategic Plan 2010–2020, once again, the government recognised the vital significance that access to safe drinking water and sanitation has on the education sector (Ministry of Education 2009).

A child's water and toilet source at home helps to predict school attendance. Calculations of GDHS data show that the time to get to the water source used by a household may affect children's schooling, as for example 6–14-year-old children who have to walk more than 30 min experience a decrease in school attendance by 12.8 % compared to those who commute less than 30 min. Even within rural areas the difference in school participation between those walking more and those less than 30 min is 11.3 % (Table 5.1). Two interrelated explanations for school participation being adversely affected by further distance to the nearest water source are that (1) it means a loss of time and energy to collect and carry water and (2) children are generally walking further to retrieve unimproved water for example from a river or lake, use of which is known to increase the propensity of sickness and disease, while data indicate that an improved water source (e.g. public standpipe or rainwater collection) is generally located at home. In terms of sanitation facilities, even 18.8 % of children from the richest quintile and 19.7 % of children in urban areas are out of school who use a bush or field as a toilet, which reflect greater shares than the national average of out-of-school children of this age at 15.6 %.

33.5 % of primary schools have no access to drinking water and 42 % have no toilets. The government's Education Strategic Plan sets the target of ensuring that all schools have access to drinking water by 2015 (Ministry of Education 2008). For the academic year 2008/09, the most water-deprived schools at the primary level were located in the Upper West region (with 45 % access) and Northern region (50 %), while over two-thirds of all schools had access to potable water in the Greater Accra (77 %), Ashanti (76 %), Western (73 %) and Central (69 %) regions. This provides further evidence of the political discrimination of the North. Figure 5.3 illustrates how some Ghanaian children without access to

Fig. 5.3 A lack of access to an improved water source at school has health and educational costs

an improved water source at school particularly in rural areas must collect water from a local pond. In terms of sanitation facilities, the Ghana Education Service—the implementation arm of the Ministry of Education—sets the norm of two urinals for each school and one toilet per 50 pupils (Netherlands Development Organisation 2008). The most sanitation-deprived schools at the primary level were located in the Northern region where 57 % of schools did not have one single toilet in 2008/09, while only 15 % of schools in the Greater Accra region did not have a functioning latrine.

Scarcity of water and toilet facilities is known to cause a higher incidence of sickness, infection and disease—the most common being diarrhoea, typhoid, cholera, guinea worm infection and Buruli Ulcer, as field research indicates. If a student does not drink sufficient water or any at all in school, this can cause dehydration and adversely affect his or her attention span and ability to retain information in class. Field research conducted in 2010 for this analysis with primary students in Accra indicates that even in the capital some schools do not have access to free potable water, and interviewed students were required to pay 5 pesewas (local currency) per half litre water sachet (about US$0.03 at 2010 exchange rates). It also found that even in the centre of the capital city some schools only have limited sanitary facilities deemed for urination but no on-site toilets so that children who need to defecate either wait until school is over or are required to walk home.

In the last section of this chapter, the focus of the analysis is turned to assess how education affects health-related variables. Specifically, regression analysis is conducted to determine the impact of education on various health and social behaviours of women, ranging from fertility to malaria prevention behaviour.

Comparison of Health Outcomes by Educational Level and Cost-Benefit Analysis

This section analyses (1) the net impact of women's schooling on their health and social behaviours and (2) the health and social outcomes of each educational level and conducts a cost-benefit analysis using public costs per student for different educational cycles.

The following statistical analysis provides insight into the behavioural changes and social and health outcomes that can be attributed to different years and levels of schooling. As women climb up the educational ladder, they respond differently to health issues, independent of individual, household and community factors. Logistic and linear regressions are conducted in the following that are based on a similar model employed in Malawi (see World Bank 2010). The regressions here estimate the impact of schooling on social behaviour *ceteris paribus* (i.e. education's simulated net impact) and include the following control variables for respondents: age, geographic location (*de facto* region of residence), a health supply indicator (physical access to a health facility) and type of occupation (agriculture, sales or services). Given that

GDHS does not collect data on individuals' earnings, occupation is used here as a proxy indicator to control for different levels of wealth, as an individual's level of income is highly correlated with their occupation, on an incremental scale from occupation in agriculture, followed by sales, and finally, services (shown in Chap. 6 covering economic welfare). The simulated net impact calculated from the regression results of the econometric model are illustrated in Table 5.6, while only the first column reflects basic descriptive statistics.

The simulated net probability of a woman having received one or more tetanus injections during pregnancy is 96 % if she completes tertiary education (16 years of schooling), whereas it is 84 % if she has no formal schooling. These percentages are the likelihood for a simulated person who would have the same age, access to health facilities, physical location and occupation/wealth as an average Ghanaian woman but who would have completed tertiary education or had no schooling, respectively. In terms of malaria, results indicate that the probability of having used a drug to prevent malaria during pregnancy is 56 % for non-educated individuals, while completing a university degree explains a 24 % increase in usage, with other factors being equal. Most Ghanaian women have an antenatal visit during pregnancy and receive assistance with delivery, but more schooling improves the probability of both.

Being young at a woman's first birth raises the risk of infant and child deaths. By completing primary education, the age at which women have their first birth is delayed by 1.4 years, and if they are university graduates by 3.6 years, partly because the opportunity costs of parenthood tend to be larger among more educated women. In addition, non-educated women are likely to give birth to 4.2 children. This number decreases on average to 3.6 children for those who finish the primary cycle and to 2.5 children for university graduates. That is, completing a university degree explains a reduction of almost two childbirths per woman, with other influences constant, and as such schooling can be seen as the most effective means to reduce fertility rates in the country. While being more educated promotes lower fertility rates, giving birth to fewer children in turn has positive effects on a household's capacity to invest more in the education of each child.

Table 5.7 shows that the effect of primary schooling is strongest on the health indicators of whether women have antenatal visits, are assisted during child delivery and receive tetanus injections during pregnancy, for which over half of the benefits on these health indicators are accounted for by finishing the primary cycle. In total, completing primary school (6 years of schooling) represents 41 % of education's overall impact on health behaviours, whereas lower and upper secondary schooling (3 years each) account for 20 and 21 %, respectively, and tertiary education (4 years of schooling) for about 18 %.

Primary schooling is highly cost-efficient in improving health outcomes given low public costs per student relative to higher levels of education. The efficiency of allocated resources to primary education in increasing health outcomes is, if all costs remain equal, nearly 2 times greater than for lower secondary, 4.4 times greater than for upper secondary and 29.9 times greater than for higher education. This is relevant for public policy in that decision-makers need to be informed about which educational levels are the most resource efficient and impact health outcomes the most.

Table 5.6 Simulated net impact of years of completed education on health and social behaviours of women, 2008/09

Probability of average woman:		Basic descriptive data avg.	Non-educated	Highest year of completed education								Change explained by completing tertiary
				Primary			Secondary			Tertiary		
				2	4	6	8	10	12	14	16	
Receiving tetanus injections during pregnancy		0.88	0.84	0.86	0.88	0.90	0.92	0.93	0.94	0.95	0.96	0.12
Using vitamin A in first 2 months after delivery		0.62	0.56	0.59	0.61	0.63	0.66	0.68	0.70	0.72	0.74	0.17
Using drug to prevent malaria during pregnancy		0.63	0.56	0.59	0.62	0.65	0.68	0.71	0.74	0.77	0.79	0.24
Woman's age at her first birth, among	20–29-year olds	19.4	18.4	18.8	19.2	19.6	20.0	20.4	20.9	21.3	21.7	3.3
	40–49-year olds	21.2	21.1	21.2	21.3	21.4	21.5	21.6	21.7	21.8	–	0.8
	15–49-year olds	20.1	19.0	19.5	19.9	20.4	20.8	21.3	21.7	22.2	22.6	3.6
Having an antenatal visit during pregnancy		0.96	0.95	0.96	0.97	0.97	0.98	0.98	0.99	0.99	0.99	0.04
Using iron tablets during pregnancy		0.85	0.86	0.87	0.87	0.88	0.88	0.89	0.89	0.90	0.90	0.04
Receiving assistance with the delivery of the child		0.97	0.97	0.97	0.98	0.98	0.98	0.99	0.99	0.99	0.99	0.02
Interval between last and preceeding birth (months)		45.2	43.0	44.1	45.2	46.3	47.4	48.5	49.6	50.7	51.8	8.8
Number of children ever born, among	Women, 15–49 years old	3.7	4.2	4.0	3.8	3.6	3.4	3.2	2.9	2.7	2.5	−1.7
	Women, 45–49 years old	7.9	8.1	7.8	7.6	7.4	7.2	7.0	6.8	6.5	–	−1.6
Female literacy	15–49 years old	0.18	0.00	0.00	0.01	0.04	0.18	0.55	0.87	0.97	1.00	1.00
	15–24 years old	0.19	0.00	0.00	0.00	0.03	0.22	0.71	0.96	0.99	–	1.00

Source Author's regression results based on GDHS data

Note The data analysis refers to women between 15 and 49 years of age unless otherwise indicated. It covers 2,992 female respondents, while it is worth taking into account that behaviours are self-reported. For two of the indicators, there are no or minimal observations for women 40–49 years of age and 45–49 years of age who have 16 years of completed education, reflecting the strong gender-bias in tertiary institutions over the past which is only slowly reducing. The regression allows for non-linearity in age. Linear regression is used for the variables covering age of respondent at 1st birth, preceding birth interval in months and total children ever born, while logistic regression is used for all remaining indicators. Among the control variables applied at the individual, household and community level, education is the only one that has a positive impact on all health and social behaviours while its impact is however statistically insignificant on using iron tablets during pregnancy, on women's age at 1st birth among 40–49-year olds, and on the number of children ever born among 45–49-year olds, likely given the relatively small survey samples for these sub-groups

Table 5.7 Impact of completed level of education on various behaviours of women, as a percentage for different cycles, and cost-benefit incidence

		Primary (versus non-educated)	Lower secondary (versus primary)	Upper secondary (versus lower)	Higher education (versus upper secondary	Total
High/medium contribution of primary cycle	Having an antenatal visit during pregnancy	55.3	18.3	13.6	12.8	100
	Receiving assistance with the delivery of the child	53.7	18.3	14.0	14.0	100
	Receiving tetanus injections during pregnancy	52.2	18.6	14.7	14.6	100
Moderate contribution of primary cycle	Number of children ever born among 45–49-year olds	42.9	21.4	21.4	14.3	100
	Using drug to prevent malaria during pregnancy	42.0	19.3	17.7	21.0	100
	Using iron tablets during pregnancy	41.0	18.6	18.1	22.3	100
	Using vitamin A in first 2 months after delivery	40.3	19.0	18.1	22.6	100
	Woman's age at her first birth	37.5	18.8	18.8	25.0	100
	Interval between last and preceding birth	37.5	18.8	18.7	25.0	100
	Increasing female literacy	3.8	30.5	53.4	12.3	100
Average social impact, by educational level		41	20	21	18	100
Average social impact, by year of educational level		6.8	6.7	7.0	4.6	
Public cost per student, by educational level (in Cedis)		548.94	494.94	1,236.99	7,064.44	
Public cost per student, by year of educational level (in Cedis)		91.49	164.98	412.33	1,766.11	
Efficiency (= impact/spending)		0.0747	0.0404	0.0170	0.0025	

Source Author's calculations based on results from Table 5.6 together with government expenditure data for the latest year available, 2006 (Preliminary Education Sector Performance Report, MOESS 2009)

Note To calculate the impact of a completed level of education on a given health indicator, the methodology used here subtracts the respective impact for the last year of a given level of education from that for the last year of the previous level of education and then divides this value by the overall change between no education and the last year of higher education

Conclusion and Policy Implications: The Intersectorality of Health and Education

This chapter analysed the interlocking and complementary nature of health and education, with a particular focus on identifying the interdependencies and forms of relationships between universal primary completion (MDG2) and various health MDGs—malnutrition (MDG1), maternal health (MDG5), malaria and HIV (MDG6) and water and sanitation (MDG7). By establishing hotspots of low MDG performance and the extent of their low performance, specific policy, organisational and investment priorities can be identified.

A child's health status influences enrolment, absenteeism and completion—early in life. Pockets of children in Ghana are educationally vulnerable due to a number of health hazards, the main causes of which are: (1) current high levels of chronically undernourished and short/stunted children under-5 at 28 % of this population and most young children and many youth suffering from anaemia, (2) the likelihood of children 6–14 years of age attending school reducing by 1.7 % nationally and by 6.3 % in the North if they did not sleep under a mosquito net the night before the survey while taking into account that the rural poor are the most frequent bed net users (GDHS 2008/09), (3) about 1.5 % of children 0–14 years of age having lost one or both parents due to AIDS by 2009 (UNAIDS 2010) and (4) an unfavourable school environment where in the academic year 2008/09 about 42 % of primary schools had no on-site toilets and 33.5 % had no access to potable water, affecting about 1.6 and 1.2 million children, respectively (EMIS data). Younger children (6–7-year olds) tend to be most disadvantaged as a result of health and sanitation conditions. The mechanisms through which a child's poor health status and environment affect late enrolment, absenteeism and lower school retention appear to be related to growth retardation (mental and physical stunting), increased susceptibility to infection and delayed recovery from sickness (higher likelihood of a deficient immune system), fever and fatigue, dehydration (reduced concentration and information retention), lower levels of energy and motivation and poor hygiene standards (illness and disease). The combination of poor health and education outcomes also has enduring effects on a child's prospects later in life.

The level of education that an individual acquires influences their health status—later in life. In a circular relationship, those who acquire more schooling react differently to specific situations, whether regarding pregnancy, nutrition, malaria, HIV/AIDS or other health-related issues. In terms of fertility, a mother's educational profile largely shapes contraceptive use, child-bearing behaviour including postponed childbirth and, among others, the number of children one gives birth to. One example of the educational effects on fertility is that mothers 15–49 years of age with 10 or more living children have either no schooling or only incomplete primary, and no mother with more than 6 children has any higher education based on 2008/09 GDHS data calculations. Moreover, regression analysis conducted here supports the view that the national fertility rate could be strongly reduced if all Ghanaians received secondary schooling and almost halved if they received higher education.

It cannot be emphasised enough that a critical concern of the sector is to ensure children begin primary school at the official age of six, which appears strongly dependent upon reducing current levels of child stunting and thus malnutrition and especially anaemia, from which the majority of Ghanaian children suffer. A child's nutritional status has therefore been identified as one of the most important external influences shaping the educational landscape in Ghana. Finally, if continued progress is made on these fronts and all children complete at least basic schooling, this would not only yield high health and social returns but also yield high economic returns.

Chapter 6
Economics of Education: Household Welfare, Poverty and Child Labour

A central aim of the Government of Ghana "is to have a civil, affordable, quality education at all levels, but in particular at the basic school level, where life really begins", as cited in the interview with the Minister of Education in late 2010. Education is, however, still not civil (universal) and remains unaffordable for many of the well over a million children of basic school-age who are at the periphery of the school system often due to direct and indirect costs as well as associated opportunity costs of schooling. This chapter sheds light on the interrelationships between schooling, poverty and child labour. It explores the basic question of how widespread levels of poverty and income inequalities across the country affect the demand for, supply of and exclusion from educational services. It also examines, on the same token, the extent to which one's educational status influences how much one earns later in life, analysing not only the private but also public rate of return to education. Finally, by applying descriptive statistics and regression analysis it takes a particular focus on identifying the determinants of child labour and school participation and their interactions with and consequences on each other, from the findings of which a number of policy options to combat child labour and increase schooling opportunities are derived and discussed.

Geographic isolation is a good proxy indicator for extreme income poverty. It is important to highlight at the beginning of this chapter that spatial and income disparities in Ghana are highly interlinked, as data below illustrates that geographically isolated groups are commonly also the most socioeconomically deprived. It is therefore necessary to bear in mind several critical points throughout this chapter. The accumulation of adverse interlocking conditions afflicting the North (lower levels of human capital, population density, basic infrastructure, soil fertility etc.) contributes to lower standards of welfare in this part of the country. It is argued here that development economists have for too long overplayed the significance of the role of monetary poverty in explaining educational poverty. The analysis here breaks away from this conventional thinking and stresses the point that having lower levels of income does not generally lead people to live in less favourable geographic conditions, but empirical evidence seems to support the contrary, with GLSS data for 2005/06 indicating that the Upper East, Upper West and Northern regions are home to all districts that fall into the bottom quintile.

A. Krauss, *External Influences and the Educational Landscape*,
SpringerBriefs in Economics, DOI: 10.1007/978-1-4614-4936-2_6,

Poverty reduction, in absolute and relative terms, has been rapid but mainly pro-South. During 1992–2006, the population of Ghana grew by 6.9 million, while 1.6 million people escaped poverty (measured by per capita consumption levels or the equivalent of US$1.08 per day using 2009 prices) (World Bank 2010d). From a North–South perspective, this remarkable achievement becomes a success story of the South, where 2.5 million people moved out of poverty whereas the number of poor increased by 0.9 million in the North. Thus, over this period the share of people living in poverty dropped from 48 to 20 % in the South; though in the North it only reduced from 69 to 63 %. In absolute terms, while 7.9 million Ghanaians lived in poverty in 1992, 6.3 million did in 2006, with the national share reducing from about one in every two people (51.7 %) to almost one in every four people (28.5 %) over the period (ibid.). Ghana is one of only a select few African countries on track for the 1st MDG of halving, between 1990 and 2015, the share of people who live in poverty based on Africa Development data. Projections indicate that poverty, if demographic and economic trends remain constant, will likely affect about 40 % of the North's population by 2030 while it is nearly eradicated in the South (World Bank 2010d). From a public finance perspective, it is critical to reduce poverty in the country as the poor make insignificant tax contributions, if any at all, which limits the capacity of public investment in education.

Economic Background Characteristics: Effects on Access and Outcomes

For many poor households living under harsh and deprived conditions, there is no margin of income above subsistence that can be channelled into future investments in the human capital assets of household members. Table 6.1 illustrates that the costs which fall on households to participate in schooling represent a financial obstacle for the most disadvantaged, given that 44.3 % of adults aged 18 or older have not even finished the primary cycle who come from the bottom quintile while only 5 % did not in the top quintile. The more limited supply of educational services in rural and Northern areas, where the poor are highly concentrated, nonetheless helps to explain this disparity.

Educational mobility: attainment is economically stratified at each higher level. Beyond the resource pool available to households, the government itself also carries a large financial burden in delivering tertiary education in the country, with public spending on the average Ghanaian tertiary student totalling 213.4 % of GDP per capita annually based on 2008 Africa Development data. Tertiary education in Ghana is viewed as an institution from which economically disenfranchised segments of society are almost entirely excluded. The poor (those from the bottom two quintiles) account for only 6 % of Ghanaians with higher education compared to 90.1 % stemming from the top two quintiles (Table 6.1). Furthermore, only 1.3 % of female tertiary graduates come from the poorest two quintiles (and none from the North).

Table 6.1 Educational and skills status of adults 18 years of age or older by quintile levels, 2008/09

Skills level/completed level of education		Average	Quintile level 1	2	3	4	5	Total	Number of observations
Unskilled	No schooling	43.4	44.3	23.1	16.9	10.6	5.0	100	10,670
	Primary	10.8	19.9	25.6	22.8	20.4	11.3	100	2,654
	Lower secondary	28.8	7.4	17.9	22.2	28.2	24.4	100	7,087
Semi-/skilled	Upper secondary	14.9	3.8	6.9	12.0	24.6	52.8	100	3,674
Highly-/skilled	Tertiary	2.1	2.0	4.0	4.0	14.0	76.1	100	506

Source Author's calculations based on GDHS data
Note The survey sample covers 24,591 respondents

Implementing the 'free' element of fcuBE, which implies that all children are to have access to basic schooling irrespective of coming from the poorest or richest groups in society, faces large constraints. It is likely that the educational profile of an adult today bears some relation to the wealth of the household in which he or she grew up and so may partly be co-determined with past consumption of education services. One can conclude from Table 6.2 that, because school participation is closely associated with welfare levels at home, many households have the desire to ensure their children attend school provided that resources allow for it.

Children in households with agricultural land or livestock are twice as likely to be out of school. A very significant finding is that most 6–14-year-old children live in households owning land used for agriculture (62.8 %) or owning livestock, herds or farm animals (61 %), whose chances of not participating in school are almost two times as high compared to those who live in households without these assets—and even increases in the North. This statistical evidence suggests that the opportunity costs for schooling are, when households own agricultural land and/or livestock, generally high due to the direct need to assist parents on the farm. The data here supports the basic argument made in Chap. 3 covering macroeconomics that the country's strong dependency on agriculture helps to crowd out human resources by placing less demand on education.

Out-Of-Pocket Expenditure (Private Costs) for Education

There are not only public costs for education, encompassing governmental funding for teacher salaries, school infrastructure, teacher training and so forth, but also private costs that fall on households (registration fees, uniforms, transport, school lunches etc.). Initially in 1961 a fee-free policy was implemented in

Table 6.2 Share of children aged 6–14 who did not attend school in the academic year 2008/09, by various economic background characteristics and (dis-) advantaged groups

All shares refer to school non-attendance rates out of 100 %	Total	North	South	Rural	Urban	Poorest quintile	Richest quintile	Girl	Boy	Total observations
Total	15.6	28.4	9.3	18.9	9.6	29.4	7.4	15.2	15.9	11,589
Quintile 1 (poorest)	29.4	33.8	18.1	29.1	36.9	–	–	29.1	29.6	3,477
Quintile 2	13.8	24.6	10.2	13.6	15.4	–	–	13.0	14.5	2,451
Quintile 3	9.2	16.2	7.9	8.0	10.7	–	–	9.5	8.9	2,132
Quintile 4	6.9	7.6	6.8	6.5	7.0	–	–	6.7	7.1	1,881
Quintile 5 (richest)	7.4	12.1	6.9	3.1	8.0	–	–	9.4	5.2	1,648
Household owns land used for agriculture	18.6	30.6	9.8	20.0	12.6	29.8	7.4	17.9	19.2	7,274
Household owns no land used for agriculture	10.5	19.3	8.7	14.8	8.2	25.9	7.4	11.0	10.0	4,315
Household owns livestock, herds or farm animals	18.8	30.2	10.0	20.4	12.0	30.1	6.2	18.2	19.2	7,071
Household owns no livestock, herds or farm animals	10.6	20.8	8.6	14.0	8.3	24.7	7.8	11.0	10.2	4,518
Has electricity at home	7.7	12.7	6.8	7.0	8.1	17.5	7.3	8.1	7.4	5,357
Has no electricity at home	22.4	32.9	12.8	23.2	16.3	29.7	12.5	21.9	22.8	6,230
Has a computer at home	7.3	15.6	6.0	7.1	7.3	0.0	7.2	11.7	2.9	480
Has no computer at home	16.0	28.6	9.5	19.0	9.9	29.4	7.5	15.4	16.5	11,100

Source Author's calculations based on GDHS data

Note Data for children in households owning a computer within the poorest quintile covers a limited number of observations and should be read with caution

Ghana but later reversed due to economically difficult times (World Bank and UNICEF 2009), then applied again under the fcuBE reforms in 1996 that were not achieved by the target year 2006, and finally to try and compensate for these inadequate efforts the capitation grant was introduced in 2004/05, the limitations of which are critically discussed in Chap. 8.

Household and school survey data collected in Ghana by the World Bank (2004a) established that 45.9 % of parents consider the (in-)direct and opportunity costs of education as the main reason for children's non-participation in school, rising to 78.2 % among head-teachers. This survey, which also asked parents why their 6–21-year-old children dropped out of school, revealed that 35 % were not able to cover school costs and/or there was a need for their children to assist with familial tasks and income generation (ibid.).

Households spend on average about US$60–100 per primary and lower secondary student annually. GLSS 2005/06 asks household respondents 'how much was spent on education in the past twelve months', which could be used as a proxy indicator to measure the extent to which the government is able or not able to deliver 'free basic schooling' to its citizens. The annual household expenditure on education for the average primary student—given an exchange rate of US$1.00 to GH¢0.92 (in new Cedis) in 2006—was US$57.40 (GH¢52.81). Education expenditure therefore accounts for an important share of the average household income at US$1,327 or per capita income at US$433 for the same year. The fact that multiple school-age children and youth live in most households multiplies this already substantial share of household expenditure for education. And, in spite of the rhetoric of 'free basic education', households still pay 57.7 % of the amount that the government does to send a child to primary school and actually spend much more than the government at all pre-tertiary levels of education when including the opportunity costs (forgone earnings) associated with schooling, as Table 6.4 later shows. Beyond the statistical evidence, a nuanced interpretation of the barriers to schooling that fees present was given by the Minister of Education during the interview in 2010 for this analysis, stating that many parents:

> need to put themselves in a position to provide some pocket money for the children to take to school and have a breakfast. They need to prepare breakfast for them if they are in that position to do so. [...] they have to provide not only the uniform but sandals or a school bag, a slate or some other learning material that should be made available to the child. Because of the poverty, most of them [parents of out-of-school children] cannot do this, and therefore the urge to send the children to school is not there. It is not there.

Field research conducted in 2010 for this analysis with upper secondary students in Accra indicates that some students interviewed dropped out of school temporarily solely because school fees were too expensive, in some cases because they increased by up to 40 % over the course of one year (much higher than levels of inflation for recent years). Some parents though who perceive post-basic education to be unattainable for their children due to the associated expenses may be less inclined to send their children to primary or lower secondary at all, given that prospects of being able to finance schooling at each higher level are incrementally scarce.

Because current financial assets of households help to determine current consumption levels, the acquisition of educational assets in the past is likely to have been determined by past educational consumption and thus by past welfare levels. These forms of endogeneity are not insignificant explanations for the intergenerational persistence of poverty—both monetary and educational—and justify further public sector intervention wherever public or private provision of educational goods and services is either lacking or unaffordable throughout the country.

Levels of Education: Effects on Income

A Ghanaian's income level increases exponentially according to his or her educational status. A lack of investment or insufficient investment in education can deprive a child or young person of one of the most effective mechanisms to improve their capacities, ensure productive employment and enhance levels of income later in life. Table 6.3 crosses GLSS data on income earned from employment by household heads 15 years of age or older with their respective levels of education and skills. Unskilled Ghanaians earn annually considerably less than their semi-skilled (/skilled) counterparts, following an earnings scale of GH¢117 (US$127) for those who have no schooling, GH¢168 (US$183) among primary completers and GH¢339 (US$368) for basic school graduates compared to GH¢702 (US$763) and GH¢1,040 (US$1,130) for upper secondary and TVET graduates, respectively. A university graduate, depending on whether female or male, earns an average of GH¢2,760 and GH¢3,410, respectively (Table 6.3). Earnings for tertiary degree holders, which are 28.7 times the amount than for the non-educated, provide evidence of the very large demand among employers for (highly-) skilled workers in the labour force in Ghana. From a political economy perspective, the populist regimes that delivered mass education were also largely anti-elite and so suppressed higher education which likely contributes to today's unmet demand for highly skilled workers.

In Northern Ghana returns to education are lower largely due to over 70 % *of its population having agricultural livelihoods.* Relative to no schooling, completing the primary cycle in the North is associated with a minimal rise in income—GH¢63 (US$68) compared to GH¢77 (US$84)—while increases are larger in the South (Table 6.3). This raises an important public policy concern since about half of Northerners 15–19 years old have not been able to complete a full course of primary schooling (compared to only about one in five in the South) based on GDHS data for 2008/09. The limited influence of formal primary schooling within the North on increased earnings can be explained by several reasons. First, over 70 % of the working population within this part of the country is engaged in agriculture and earns about GH¢50 annually irrespective if they finish 9 years of schooling or not. Second, field research in 2010 in Ghana indicates that skills and competencies are largely attained through 'learning by doing' in agriculture. Third, although educational opportunities in the North have begun

Table 6.3 Annual income for household heads aged 15 or older relative to their level of skills/education attained, by various categories, 2005/06

GH¢ (new cedis) /*US$*		Level of skills/education acquired:						Average	Number of observations
		Unskilled			Semi-skilled (/skilled)		(Highly-) skilled		
		No education	Primary	Lower secondary	Upper secondary	TVET	Higher education		
Total	GH¢	117	168	339	702	1,040	3,360	476	7,668
	US$	127	183	368	763	1,130	3,652	518	
Sex									
Female	GH¢	70	78	166	443	805	2,760	216	2,088
	US$	77	84	180	481	875	3,000	234	
Male	GH¢	143	213	385	742	1,120	3,410	561	5,580
	US$	156	231	419	806	1,217	3,707	610	
Geographic location									
North	GH¢	63	77	375	603	1,240	2,920	461	2,046
	US$	68	84	407	655	1,348	3,174	501	
South	GH¢	132	177	338	739	1,020	3,470	479	5,495
	US$	143	193	368	803	1,109	3,772	520	
Rural-North	GH¢	42	96	165	238	651	2,600	142	1,618
	US$	46	105	179	259	707	2,826	154	
Rural-South	GH¢	95	136	182	434	686	3,040	217	2,759
	US$	103	148	197	472	746	3,304	236	
Urban-North	GH¢	155	264	676	837	1,540	2,980	955	428
	US$	169	287	734	910	1,674	3,239	1,038	
Urban-South	GH¢	206	235	478	821	1,100	3,550	705	2,736
	US$	224	255	520	892	1,196	3,859	766	
Age groups									
15–59	GH¢	127	175	341	713	1,080	3,290	482	6,033
	US$	138	190	371	775	1,174	3,576	524	

(continued)

Table 6.3 (continued)

GH¢ (new cedis) /*US$*		Level of skills/education acquired:						Average	Number of observations
		Unskilled			Semi-skilled (/skilled)		(Highly-) skilled		
		No education	Primary	Lower secondary	Upper secondary	TVET	Higher education		
24–59	GH¢	120	181	351	752	1,100	3,290	502	5,750
	US$	131	197	381	817	1,196	3,576	545	
45–59	GH¢	97	155	376	986	1,380	3,920	607	2,161
	US$	105	169	408	1,072	1,500	4,261	660	
Occupational group									
Public	GH¢	359	693	1,120	1,620	1,950	3,710	1,960	565
	US$	390	754	1,217	1,761	2,120	4,033	2,130	
Wage private formal	GH¢	778	768	1,040	1,280	1,760	4,770	1,370	613
	US$	846	835	1,130	1,391	1,913	5,185	1,489	
Wage private informal	GH¢	700	709	830	811	1,150	4,430	849	544
	US$	760	771	902	882	1,250	4,815	923	
Self-employed, agriculture	GH¢	54	44	52	108	201	1,330	625	3,603
	US$	59	47	56	117	218	1,446	680	
Self-employed, business (non-agri.)	GH¢	31	62	139	206	310	2,270	170	1,890
	US$	33	67	151	224	337	2,467	184	

Source Author's calculations based on GLSS data

Note In terms of exchange rate calculations, the GLSS data set uses old cedis while 10,000 old cedis equals 1 new cedi, with the average exchange rate at GH¢0.92 (¢9,176.48) to one US dollar as of 2006 (GLSS 2008). Income is measured here as income from employment, which better captures actual earnings related to one's level of schooling attained compared to using all sources of household income including income from agricultural and non-farm activities, rent, remittances and other sources. No schooling completed refers to individuals ranging from those without any schooling at all to those who may have reached the 5th year but did not finish primary school. Completion of lower secondary reflects either recipients of the middle school leaving certificate (MSLC) or the basic education certificate examination (BECE). Upper secondary includes those who completed the senior secondary certificate examination (SSCE) and, for older respondents, O-levels or A-levels. Tertiary education includes university graduates and post graduate degree holders. In terms of data for occupational groups, 6 % of respondents (453 individuals in total) are not working, for whom data is missing and calculations are not possible. Finally, data for employment in agriculture has been merged to refer to engagement in either crop or export agriculture opening from very low levels, higher completion rates do not appear to have led to many alternative options to agricultural livelihoods. One policy implication is that interventions supporting primary schooling will have to be complemented with opening access to other educational levels and with other policy instruments to widen the formal job market for Northerners. Another policy implication is that if future rewards for attending and completing primary schooling among the most disadvantaged are not eventually increased, the poverty-reducing potential of education policy may be undermined.

Private and Social Rates of Return to Education

Individuals—and society as a whole—benefit economically from educational investments in Ghana. For many households, the decision to send a child or adolescent to school and for what duration may be assessed using cost-benefit analysis, comparing the direct and opportunity costs of schooling on one hand with the future economic benefits to the household, including income returns, on the other. Many people invest in their children's educational capital and at times their own—an added year or cycle of education—provided that the marginal value of the investment surpasses its additional expenses. This is, as shown in the following, clearly the case in Ghana.

The private and social rates of return, while very low for primary school, are particularly high for tertiary schooling. Table 6.4 calculates the private rate of return (RoR) denoted as the additional share of earnings on average that a Ghanaian gains by acquiring more schooling relative to the household expenditures accrued for his or her schooling, calculating also the foregone income as a result of pursuing additional years of education instead of working (see table for methodology). The cost-benefit analysis conducted here reveals large private rates of return in the country particularly at higher levels of schooling, at 5 % for primary education and at about 20 % for secondary schooling, increasing to 67.5 % for higher education. The social rate of return divides the extra income received for a given level by the total expenses for schooling at that level, including both public and private expenses, and therefore reflects the marginal benefits for society. The social rate of return to education in Ghana, which is by definition lower than the private rate of return, ranges from 3.3 % for primary school and consequently 13.5 and 12.1 % for lower and upper secondary, respectively, to 24.2 % for higher education.

Child Labour

Immediate or postponed gratification: interconnections between child labour and schooling. At times high fees for education can push children prematurely into the labour force, sometimes to be able to finance school, or pull children

Table 6.4 Private and social rates of return to education in Ghana, 2005/06

Amounts are in GH¢	Income earned by adults		Public cost per student		Private cost per student				Rate of return	
	Annual income (GLSS 2006)	Additional annual income compared to previous level (primary compared to no schooling) (GLSS 2006)	Annual cost (Gov. data for 2006)	Cost for the entire level (Gov. data for 2006)	Annual cost (GLSS 2006)	Cost for the entire level (GLSS 2006)	Total cost for the entire level (direct cost + foregone earnings) (GLSS 2006)	Total social cost for the entire level (public + total private)	Total private RoR (%)	Total social RoR (%)
Primary schooling	168	51	91.49	548.94	52.81	316.86	1,018.86	1,567.80	5.0	3.3
Lower secondary	339	171	164.98	494.94	88.83	266.49	770.49	1,265.43	22.2	13.5
Upper secondary	702	363	412.33	1,236.99	244.65	733.95	1,750.95	2,987.94	20.7	12.1
Higher education	3,360	2,658	1,766.11	7,064.44	457.26	1,829.04	3,935.04	10,999.48	67.5	24.2

Source Author's calculations based on GLSS data and on administrative expenditure data for 2006 (Preliminary Education Sector Performance Report, Ministry of Education 2008)

Note Unemployed individuals are not considered in the tabulations, given that being unemployed is generally not a permanent status while it is even conceivable that during a phase of unemployment people still generate some form of income. Public and private costs are computed by multiplying the annual unit cost per student by the number of years of schooling within the given level of education. The public cost per student reflects the total government expenditure at a given level of education divided by public enrolment figures at that level. Forgone earnings are calculated by multiplying the number of years of schooling for a given level by the earnings that the previous level would have yielded if studies were not pursued. The total private RoR for primary schooling, for example, is calculated as follows: GH¢51 (additional annual income) divided by GH¢1,018.86 (the total private cost per student) equals 5.0 %. The total social RoR is calculated in the same way but the public cost is added to the total private cost out of school because of a lack of funding. Often children, however, need to work irrespective of the direct and indirect costs of schooling, since time is money and opportunity costs of children increase as they get older. For many economically vulnerable households in Ghana, the demand for schooling therefore competes with the demand for child labour, especially given that the majority of households in the country rely on labour-intensive agricultural livelihoods for subsistence. Parents gain in the short-term from children who work through their contribution to earnings and at the same time they can save on costs for education if their children do not attend school. In the long-term, however, children who work generally earn less later in life as a consequence of a weaker educational background, as Table 6.3 illustrated above.

ILO (2008) differentiates between unharmful (or less harmful) 'child work' and more harmful 'child labour', with the latter defined broadly as the engagement of children under the age of 15 on a regular basis in prohibited work in order to make a living or compliment household earnings, either as a wage worker or through self employment. The former in Ghana is typically related to the assistance with (non-economic) household activities before and after school, on weekends and during holidays such as fetching water and/or wood, cooking, looking after siblings and similar chores. Evidence from field research in 2010 indicates that all children interviewed contribute in one way or another to household tasks, which are commonly seen as an inevitable part of everyday life in Ghana, not only in rural areas. In this analysis, a definition of child labour is adopted in line with the ILO definition that is used by GLSS and therefore endorsed by the government: a child is employed if he or she did "any work for pay, profit, family gain or produce anything for barter or home use during the last 7 days" (GLSS 2008).

Over the period 1992–2006 the share of child labourers aged 6–14 fell from 28 to 15.6 %. About one in every six children of primary and lower secondary age are still employed in child labour in 2005/06, amounting to about 317,000 children of this age active in the labour market based on calculations of government population/EMIS and GLSS data. Geographic location, once again, has much explanatory value. Child labour is pervasive in the North, where over four times the share of 6–14 year old children are actively employed relative to the South (33.1 % compared to 7.8 %, respectively). 53.7 % of children aged 6–14 not in school are engaged in labour activities in the North compared to 33.3 % in the South. In the Upper West region, only two-thirds of children of this age participated in school (66.9 %) and almost half engaged in labour activities (44.7 %), while at the other end of the spectrum almost all children in the Ashanti region participated in school (96.9 %) and child labour is almost nonexistent there (2.9 %).

Child labour as a form of exploitation or rather a basic component of socialisation? For many Ghanaians, child labour is seen as part of a child's socialisation process to the effect that working, as opposed to schooling, helps children get better accustomed to the skills needed later for employment. The Minister of Education appears to also culturally relativise child labour as part of life for many farming families and stated that:

> what is happening is that some parents still want to engage their children as a way of training them for the future in the occupations in which they are, at the moment, engaged. I belong to the old school, where you 'bring up the child the way he should go' so that if you are a child in a farming family you should be able to learn about farming from your parents.

Child labour and schooling are not mutually exclusive: *8.6 % of all 6–14-year olds do both.* Households do not always have to make decisions in favour of child labour and against schooling or vice versa. Rather, they are able to decide between one of four choices in relation to their children's work and schooling: 77.2 % of children 6–14 years of age are schooling and not employed, 8.6 % are simultaneously employed and schooling and 7 % are employed but not schooling, while the remaining 7.2 % are neither employed nor schooling (classified as being idle). Child labour is therefore the leading alternative to schooling but almost one in ten children of this age in Ghana are able to combine the two. The fact that only 1.6 % of Southern children are working while not schooling compared to 18.9 % of Northern children evidences the extent of the latter group's extreme marginalisation (Table 6.5). Involvement in labour activities is not inevitably a contradiction to going to school as earnings gained from employment are used at times to compensate educational costs (Fig. 6.1).

There are intergenerational effects on child labour and schooling. Table 6.5 matches the employment status of 6–14-year olds with data on their attendance in school and crosses this information with a number of their background and labour-specific characteristics. 93.7 % of child labourers are employed in (unpaid) agriculture, with the remaining 6.3 % engaged in non-agricultural employment. For the most at risk and those living at the level of subsistence, the decision can be very difficult: a family that decides to send their children to

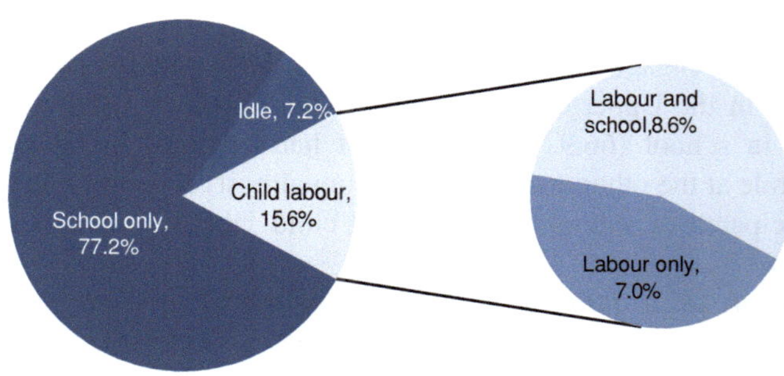

Fig. 6.1 School and labour participation rates for 6–14 year old children, 2005/06
Source Author's illustration based on calculations of data from GLSS

Fig. 6.2 Forms of child work and child labour with different degrees of hazard in Ghana

school and subsequently lacks sufficient labour on the farm and has a poor harvest could potentially even experience an unexpected and negative impact from schooling. This is an important point as it implies that for very deprived families with subsistence farming livelihoods to send all children to school may not always be a viable option in the short-term and that schooling combined with labour can still be positive if the alternative is to only be working on the farm.

Once children are physically bigger, their usefulness or value around the household and community increases: evidenced by an incremental rise in child employment from 9.9 % for 6–8-year olds to 15.4 % for 9–11-year olds followed by 19.6 % for 12–14-year olds. To offer insight into a few of the faces behind the descriptive data, Fig. 6.2 illustrates various forms of child work and labour in Ghana with different degrees of hazard, ranging from children who assist parents collecting wood or work seasonally in small-scale agriculture to those who chase tro-tros (mini-buses) in motion to sell products like fan-ice (ice-cream) and others who are exploited full-time or engaged in bondage-labour within fishing communities along the shores of Lake Volta, as participatory observations in 2010 indicate.

Opportunity costs need to be identified and tackled for education to be truly free. The removal of cost barriers alone (although a vital step) is likely to amount to an inadequate incentive for most agrarian households whose opportunity costs of schooling are comparatively high. The issue of opportunity costs is one that was highlighted in the interview with the Minister of Education, who stated that "most of the parents do not think that it is easy for them to [...] do away with the services [...] even at that tender age of 5–6 years, some of them [parents] receive services, petty–petty services, from these little children".

Table 6.5 School and labour participation rates for 6–14 year old children, 2005/06

	School, with		No schooling, with		Total	Number of observations	School	Work	
	No work	Work	No work	Work					
Total	77.2	8.6	7.2	7.0	100	7,694	85.8	15.6	←
	All shares refer to school or labour participation rates out of 100 %						*Shares are not to add up to 100 %*		
Gender									Typical profile of a child labourer (whether also schooling or not) in the last column
Female	78.0	7.9	7.7	6.4	100	3,716	85.9	14.3	
Male	76.4	9.3	6.8	7.5	100	3,978	85.7	16.8	
Age									
6–8	78.0	5.0	12.1	4.9	100	1,968	83.0	9.9	
9–11	77.6	8.7	7.0	6.7	100	2,832	86.3	15.4	
12–14	76.2	11.0	4.3	8.5	100	2,894	87.2	19.6	
Location									
North	50.6	14.1	16.3	18.9	100	2,366	64.8	33.1	
South	89.0	6.2	3.2	1.6	100	5,264	95.2	7.8	
Region									
Western	93.1	3.8	2.7	0.4	100	706	96.9	4.3	
Central	94.5	2.5	1.9	1.1	100	565	97.0	3.5	
Greater Accra	92.0	3.2	4.6	0.2	100	585	95.2	3.4	
Volta	80.4	7.1	6.8	5.7	100	674	87.5	12.8	
Eastern	78.1	19.1	1.9	0.9	100	790	97.2	20.0	
Ashanti	94.6	2.3	2.4	0.7	100	1,327	96.9	2.9	
Brong Ahafo	87.8	6.0	2.9	3.2	100	617	93.8	9.2	
Northern	54.5	8.8	15.1	21.6	100	963	63.3	30.4	
Upper east	52.2	12.3	23.2	12.3	100	684	64.5	24.6	
Upper west	43.9	23.0	11.4	21.7	100	719	66.9	44.7	
Father's level of education									
No schooling	66.6	13.1	10.1	10.2	100	994	79.7	23.3	
Primary	88.4	6.6	1.7	3.3	100	181	95.0	9.9	
Lower secondary	93.0	5.3	1.1	0.6	100	972	98.3	5.9	
Upper secondary	97.6	0.6	1.8	0.0	100	167	98.2	0.6	

(continued)

Table 6.5 (continued)

	School, with		No schooling, with		Total	Number of observations	School	Work
	No work	Work	No work	Work				
Tertiary	98.2	1.8	0.0	0.0	100	55	100	1.8
School location								
Time to and from school, 0–59 min	91.5	8.5	–	–	100	4,915	100	8.5
Time to and from school,60–119 min	89.0	11.0	–	–	100	1,094	100	11.0
Time to and from school, 120+ min	84.6	15.4	–	–	100	391	100	15.4
School participation rate by hours of class attended last week								
24 h or less	86.9	13.1	–	–	100	1,180	100	13.1
Between 25 and 34 h	91.9	8.1	–	–	100	2,650	100	8.1
35 h or more	94.1	5.9	–	–	100	1,306	100	5.9
School participation rate by hours spent on homework done								
Less than one hour	88.9	11.1	–	–	100	4,737	100	11.1
One or more hours	96.1	3.9	–	–	100	1,605	100	3.9
Shares or figures are not necessarily to add up to 100 %								
Avg. number of hours worked in week	–	19.9 h	–	34.1 h	–	1,199	–	26.3 h
Share who received payment for work	–	3.8	–	3.9	–	1,199	–	3.8
Child labour type								
Employment in agriculture, unpaid work	–	92.6	–	95.1	–	1,125	–	93.7
Employment in non-agriculture	–	7.4	–	4.9	–	76	–	6.3
Work place in village or town								
Yes	–	94.4	–	89.2	–	1,106	–	92.1
No	–	5.6	–	10.8	–	95	–	7.9

Source Author's calculations based on GLSS data

Note Children who were on school holiday during data collection have been omitted from the analysis. Data that refers to fathers with tertiary education should be read with caution given the limited number of observations

Regression Analysis on School and Labour Participation in Ghana: Establishing Determinants

This section turns to regression analysis, controlling for the presence of individual, parent, household, regional and cluster determinants, to help further understand the underlying forces pulling and pushing child labour and schooling in the country. Regressions are conducted here applying variables available in the latest survey data set on child labour (GLSS 2005/06) and influenced by variables that previous research has found to affect school and labour involvement, to a large extent based on a similar model employed in Ghana by the World Bank using data from the late 1980s and early 1990s (see Canagarajah and Coulombe 1997). Given that schooling and working are two interdependent decisions (not mutually exclusive as shown above), a bivariate probit model is applied which permits interconnected relationships between these two dependent variables, with school participation defined as "having attended school" and labour participation defined as doing "any work for pay, profit, family gain or produce anything for barter or home use during the last 7 days" (GLSS 2008).

The benefit of this statistical model is that the impacts of many influencing factors discussed throughout the analysis are considered simultaneously, making it possible to better discern among the most important influencers comparing the size and significance levels of the effects. The first model assesses the impact of demand variables on influencing household choices in favour of or against child labour and schooling, while the second model is similar but also takes into account supply variables such as distance to the nearest school facility and total school expenditure. The regression results of the econometric models are presented in Table 6.6, whereas only the last column reflects basic descriptive statistics of the explanatory variables employed. Results for both models are very similar due to the limited impact of supply variables and those for the second model are described in the following for simplification purposes.

In terms of gender, regression results show that overall the difference between 6–14-year-old boys and girls is not significant in their probability of being engaged in work. This finding is consistent with previous research (Canagarajah and Coulombe 1997). Moreover, if a mother is present in the household, her child's likelihood of schooling increases by 2.5 %, with everything else (individual, household, community and cluster factors) being equal. In relation to fathers' without any schooling (the reference group), those who have at least primary education are 3–6 % more likely to send their children to school while they are 4–5 % less likely to require their children to work. This finding supports the basic argument made throughout the chapter that opening educational opportunities for children and youth is a good insurance for the schooling and non-employment of their own children later in life.

The probability of a child of primary or lower secondary age having attended school is 2–3 % higher if he or she falls into one of the top three welfare quintiles compared to the bottom quintile (the reference group). These percentages are the likelihood for a simulated child who would have the same age, physical location,

Table 6.6 Bivariate probit regression results: determinants of child labour and school participation for 6–14-year olds, 2005/06

Marginal effect reflects the share of a variable's impact. T-ratio shows if a variable's significance level is over 95 % if >1.96 or <1.96	Model 1 demand variables				Model 2 demand and supply variables				Basic descriptive data avg.
	School participation		Labour participation		School participation		Labour participation		S 0.83 L 0.17
	Marginal effect	t-ratio	Marginal effect	t-ratio	Marginal effect	t-ratio	Marginal effect	t-ratio	
Independent variables									
Child characteristics									
Age	0.383	1.41	0.657	1.72	0.368	1.47	0.609	1.58	9.7
Age[2a]	−0.235	−1.22	−0.330	−1.23	−0.219	−1.22	−0.318	−1.18	–
Male (1 if so, 0 if not) (reference group, female)	−0.015	−1.94	0.018	1.68	−0.012	−1.69	0.020	1.85	0.52
Real child (1 if relationship to head is child, 0 if not)	0.019	1.63	−0.031	−2.00	0.013	1.19	−0.025	−1.58	0.69
Parent characteristics									
Mother lives in HH (1 if so, 0 if not)	0.026	2.26	0.016	1.05	0.025	2.33	0.015	0.97	0.68
Father's education, primary (1 if so, 0 if not) (ref. group, no edu.)	0.036	4.67	−0.035	−2.33	0.039	5.85	−0.042	−3.05	0.07
Father's education, lower sec. (1 if so, 0 if not)	0.066	6.41	−0.055	−4.12	0.056	5.92	−0.054	−3.86	0.38
Father's education, upper sec. or higher (1 if so, 0 if not)	0.042	5.10	−0.054	−3.65	0.034	4.15	−0.049	−3.32	0.08
Household characteristics									
Welfare quintile 2 (1 if so, 0 if not) (ref. group, quintile1)	0.009	0.96	−0.018	−1.21	0.006	0.65	−0.013	−0.89	0.22
Welfare quintile 3 (1 if so, 0 if not)	0.020	1.96	−0.021	−1.30	0.019	2.05	−0.032	−2.08	0.20
Welfare quintile 4 (1 if so, 0 if not)	0.026	2.61	−0.031	−1.98	0.025	.64	−0.042	−2.85	0.17
Welfare quintile 5 (1 if so, 0 if not)	0.036	3.89	−0.074	−6.12	0.027	.77	−0.069	−5.70	0.13
HH occupation in non-agriculture(ref. group, agriculture)	0.015	1.65	−0.027	−2.11	0.016	1.84	−0.024	−1.86	0.46
Number of HH members aged 0–5	−0.007	−1.69	0.014	2.23	−0.007	−1.85	0.014	2.27	1.4
Number of HH members aged 6–14	0.004	1.06	0.004	0.95	0.005	1.44	0.002	0.52	6.6
Number of HH members aged 15–59	0.005	2.25	−0.003	−1.05	0.006	2.37	−0.003	−1.00	2.9
Number of HH members aged 60 or older	0.008	1.36	−0.012	−1.30	0.006	1.01	−0.008	−0.90	0.4
Regional and cluster characteristics									
Western region (1 if so, 0 if not) (ref. group, Northern region)	0.037	4.49	−0.048	−3.03	0.028	3.03	−0.040	−2.30	0.08
Central region (1 if so, 0 if not)	0.042	5.36	−0.065	−4.92	0.040	5.50	−0.074	−6.60	0.08
Accra region (1 if so, 0 if not)	0.020	1.69	−0.044	−2.51	0.008	0.53	−0.043	−2.31	0.06

(continued)

Table 6.6 (contniued)

Marginal effect reflects the share of a variable's impact. T-ratio shows if a variable's significance level is over 95 % if >1.96 or <1.96	Model 1 demand variables				Model 2 demand and supply variables				Basic descriptive data avg.
	School participation		Labour participation		School participation		Labour participation		S 0.83 L 0.17
	Marginal effect	t-ratio	Marginal effect	t-ratio	Marginal effect	t-ratio	Marginal effect	t-ratio	
Volta region (1 if so, 0 if not)	0.033	3.79	−0.038	−2.18	0.032	4.14	−0.023	−1.11	0.10
Eastern region (1 if so, 0 if not)	0.046	5.83	0.063	1.95	0.042	6.00	0.062	1.79	0.11
Ashanti region (1 if so, 0 if not)	0.054	5.89	−0.082	−5.90	0.044	4.84	−0.075	−5.10	0.16
Brong Ahafo region (1 if so, 0 if not)	0.045	6.32	−0.042	−2.51	0.039	5.67	−0.040	−2.46	0.08
Upper East region (1 if so, 0 if not)	−0.033	−1.49	0.018	0.65	−0.027	−1.34	0.028	0.97	0.11
Upper West region (1 if so, 0 if not)	−0.010	−0.59	0.138	3.18	−0.001	−0.04	0.136	3.13	0.10
Total school expenditure, lowest tercile(ref. group, highest tercile)	–	–	–	–	−0.014	−0.99	−0.012	−0.74	0.33
Total school expenditure, middle tercile	–	–	–	–	0.001	0.12	−0.022	−1.66	0.33
Distance to school, 0–29 min. (ref. group, 30 or more min.)	–	–	–	–	0.033	2.63	−0.002	−0.17	0.76
Sample size of children		2,385				2,214			

Source Author's regression results based on GLSS data calculations. Note: HH stands for household. Household occupation in (non-)agriculture is calculated to reflect if one or both parents are employed in (non-)agriculture. Given that data on household expenditure for education and distance to school are only provided for students (i.e. not for children who do not attend school), these two supply variables are calculated creating the cluster median (the average for a given geographic enumeration area used for the national census), making the assumption that educational expenses for households and school distance would be very similar within a given cluster which the data also confirms. Total school expenditure includes costs for school and registration fees; contributions to PTA; uniforms and sports clothes; books and school supplies; transportation to and from school; food, board and lodging; expenses on extra classes; and in-kind expenses. Total school expenditure is divided into terciles: the lowest school expenditure tercile reflects clusters that spent on average between GH¢0 and GH¢14.30 (new cedis), the middle school expenditure tercile spent between GH¢14.31 and GH¢43.80 and the highest school expenditure tercile between GH¢43.81 and GH¢700.00 [a]Age^2 represents age squared and is included in order for the regression to allow for nonlinearity in age. Two variables have been dropped from the model with demand and supply variables due to collinearity: if the 'father lives in the household', as results are very similar to whether the mother lives in the household, and if the 'supply variables are missing', as available information is very similar to that for a cluster on distance to school and household expenditure for schooling. From the model with only demand side variables, one variable (if the father lives in the household) has been dropped due to collinearity. To capture a larger sample of all 6–14-year-old children (increase the number of observations and the accuracy of results), mothers' level of education has been withdrawn from the initial regression design, for which effects are similar to fathers' level of education. It should also be noted that GLSS does not collect information on malnutrition and anaemia (also variables like malaria/fever) so that it is not possible to include these metrics into the regression, although earlier analysis shows that they adversely influence children's schooling based on GDHS data, which in turn does not gather data on one of the dependent variables (child labour) as well as the supply variables (school expenditure and distance) access to a school facility etc. as an average Ghanaian child but who would not live in a household falling into the bottom welfare quintile. Household welfare levels (although not always significant) have effects on child labour involvement, with children in the top quintile being about 7 % less likely to be employed compared to those in the bottom quintile. A very important finding with direct policy implications is that household welfare in Ghana appears to have a weaker effect on the prevalence of schooling and child labour than geographic location, casting doubt on the common perception that it is mainly poverty pulling children away from school and pushing them prematurely into employment.

In comparison to the Northern region (the reference group), children in the Ashanti region are 4.4 % more likely to attend school. In terms of labour participation the effect of geographic location seems very strong: children who live in the Ashanti region are 7.5 % less likely to be working compared to those in the Northern region while those in the Upper West region are 13.6 % more likely to do so, reflecting a difference of 21.1 % in the likelihood of being employed, with other factors held constant.

The school expenditure variable, which reflects potential household budget limitations in affording children's schooling, shows that higher costs associated with education appear to have an insignificant effect on schooling and labour involvement. In terms of school distance, estimations illustrate that a distance of less than 30 min (compared to the reference group of over 30 min) has a positive effect on the prevalence of schooling by about 3 % but the effect on working is insignificant. It was expected that the impact of distance on schooling and working would be larger. The results could be because distances to school in 2005/06 remain relatively long for most students largely irrespective of various background characteristics including North/South or rural/urban residency.

Other variables are included in the second model (with both demand and supply variables) to confirm robustness and test whether they impact the decision for children to engage in work or go to school. One variable that does show variance is religion, at least in terms of school participation, while the impact of different religious affiliations on working is insignificant. With all other effects remaining largely similar, results suggest that Muslims would be about 4 % more likely to ensure that their children attend school relative to animists (the reference group), while Catholics and Protestants are about 5–6 % more likely to do so, respectively (this finding nonetheless has little, if any, policy relevance). In addition, when the regression is conducted without levels of household welfare to test whether its exclusion affects the parameters of the other variables, it is established that there is nearly no change at all in the remaining parameters. Estimates of sub-groups for the full model by age (children aged 12–14 or even 10–14) constrain the sample size but disaggregation is possible for gender. In a gender split model (using both demand and supply variables), differences between boys and girls were very small for all explanatory variables with two exceptions: the impact of household welfare on girls' school attendance is insignificant, and the impact of living in the Eastern region on boys' labour is very strong and significant. Estimations of these sub-samples for gender (although these two variations arise) also verify on a whole the robustness of the findings.

Overall, the statistical analysis reveals that three of the most significant predictors in constraining school participation and determining labour participation include:

- Geographic location especially in the North;
- Having parents without any schooling, particularly fathers, followed by;
- Living in a household found in the lower welfare quintiles, particularly for boys.

A very important finding is that the regression results confirm that school context features (the school supply variables) have a limited or insignificant impact on determining school attendance in Ghana. The key policy message derived from the regression results here is that raising the demand for children's schooling (particularly in the North) is likely the most effective policy approach to both minimise the incidence of child labour in the country and help to boost its human resource development for children and young adolescents alike. And, any targeted incentive package with such an objective that does not place rural households with subsistence farming livelihoods in the forefront, with a particular emphasis on the North (and possibly on older children), is likely to fail or not achieve set targets.

Conclusion: Economics of Education, Poverty and Child Labour

Household occupation and welfare levels predict educational opportunities—early in life. This chapter highlights the value of the social and economic strata of households in helping to shape children's futures through household investments in education and the need for child labour, while finding that economic variables are very closely linked to residency in the South or in the North, which (as mentioned) is home to all districts that fall into the bottom quintile (2005/06 GLSS data). School demand is often determined by assessing the costs and benefits associated with schooling. With the average household spending US$57.40 per primary student annually, the government is not able—despite being arguably willing—to deliver 'free basic schooling' to its citizens. And it appears that as long as education is also accompanied by indirect and opportunity costs, it will remain difficult, if not impossible, to attain the other fcuBE objectives of compulsory and universal basic education. As vulnerability, related primarily to Northern residency, household occupation in subsistence farming, impoverishment and low levels of parental education, is at the root of most educational deprivation, policies that focus on raising the demand of the poor North will likely prove most effective at the current juncture of Ghana's education development.

The level of education one reaches predicts one's type of occupation and welfare level—later in life. Survey data appears to support the view that the 28.5 % of people in 2005/06 living in poverty could be strongly reduced if all children and youth would in fact receive at least basic education that the government has made compulsory. If a Ghanaian acquires more education and skills, this generally contributes to obtaining better types of employment and thus to income levels increasing exponentially, following an earnings scale of US$127 annually for household heads 15 years of age or older without any schooling to US$368 and US$763 for lower and upper secondary completers respectively and, finally, to US$3,360 for university graduates (Table 6.3). As most of the very economically vulnerable live in the North, poverty alleviation will largely be conditional on the country's capacity to promote human capital development for Northerners, while also widening the formal job market for Northerners. A cost-benefit analysis, calculating the direct and opportunity costs of schooling on one hand with the future income returns to the household on the other, reveals that the private and social rates of return for households and for society on a whole, while low for primary school, increase rapidly for secondary education and are particularly high for tertiary schooling (Table 6.4).

Equitable human resource development is out of reach with present levels of child labour. It should be of prime policy importance for the government that about 317,000 children aged 6–14 are working (15.6 % of this population). A major constraint to Ghana's economic development challenge—as argued throughout the analysis—is the country's low levels of educational capital, and as 7 % of children of this age are employed and not in school, effective interventions to tackle child labour are important for more equitable national development. The fact that the majority of out-of-school children of this age in the North are engaged in labour activities indicates that child employment is the leading alternative to schooling. Child labour has therefore been identified as one of the most important external influences shaping the educational landscape in Ghana. A very important finding of the regression analysis is that the school supply variables (school expenditure and distance) have a limited or insignificant impact on determining both school and labour participation in the country, while background characteristics have much greater impact, above all North–South residency. Given that child labour is separate from the decision to attend school for almost one in every ten children 6–14 years old in the country, opening up educational opportunities for the marginalised cannot be separate from demand-side interventions to mitigate child labour. It is important to stress this point that a supply-driven approach will very likely have much less of an impact on attracting and retaining the remaining out-of-school children (located mainly in the highly agriculture-dependent North) than a demand-driven approach with a focus on reducing the strong need for child labour. The descriptive data and regression analysis suggest that access to and completion of basic schooling will continue to be constrained until (in-)direct school costs are truly abolished, until opportunity costs are minimised and especially until the specific circumstances of child workers become reflected in the objective and content of policy reforms that need to begin targeting rural households with subsistence farming livelihoods, focusing largely on the North and especially on those at the margin of the school system (and possibly older children). The interlocking nature is evident: universalising basic education will not be possible without minimising child labour and eliminating child labour will not be possible without nearing universal basic education. This interlocking relationship is not a 'catch 22' given that public intervention in other countries has been able to simultaneously link large reductions in child labour to large increases in schooling, particularly through cash transfers to relevant households conditional on school attendance and no child labour involvement. Such a scheme has been adopted in Ghana (LEAP), the shortcomings of which are discussed in Chap. 8. In closing, conditions of living in a household with a livelihood in subsistence farming can often perpetuate cycles of educational and economic poverty, but so can living in a household with many children as some or all may receive less schooling due to the financial burden multiplied by each additional child—the focus of the analysis turns to such demographic influences in the next and final thematic chapter.

Chapter 7
Demographics: Population Growth, Household Structure and Migration Patterns

This chapter explores the nature, magnitude and consequences of a number of demographic factors on human capital endowment in Ghana. It examines the externalities of population growth and population structure on the education sector. It assesses how household demographics, such as the number, age and gender of siblings who compete over limited household resources, helps to shape the educational opportunities of young household members. Finally, it analyses migration patterns—both internal and external—and the extent of their effects on human capital flight, a loss of public education spending and remittance inflows.

Population Growth and Structure

High demographic growth has and will continue to retard the country's human development. Population growth trends—as in most developing countries—reached historical highs over the past half century in Ghana. A discussion of the proportions of children and youth gaining access to schooling tells only part of the story since in the continued presence of rapid population growth even static proportions of enrolment represent large increases in absolute numbers. Estimates suggest that the size of the Ghanaian population is five times larger in 2010 at about 24.3 million people than in 1950 at less than 5 million people. This has had implications on (1) persistent influxes of new enrolments at all levels, (2) considerable fiscal constraints and (3) very large supply demands on education personnel, infrastructure and services, as illustrated throughout the analysis. Population projections support the view that heavy demographic pressures—fertility rates at 4 children per women based on 2008/09 GDHS data—will only continue to constrain the schooling system, with population figures potentially rising to about 45.2 million by 2050 (UN Population Statistics). If current demographic growth patterns especially in the poorest areas are not reduced, it is probable that smaller investments will have to be made in the education and health of each child and it is probable that this will translate into lower standards of living for many Ghanaians in these areas.

Twenty five percent of the population in Ghana is between 5 *and* 14 *years old.* The share of 0–14-year olds reflects 39 % of the entire population in Ghana (the global average is 27 %), i.e. over 9 million children are of basic education age or below and will place sustained pressure on increased physical, human and

A. Krauss, *External Influences and the Educational Landscape*,
SpringerBriefs in Economics, DOI: 10.1007/978-1-4614-4936-2_7,

Table 7.1 Trends in school enrolments, 2001/02–2009/10

	Years		Increase over period (as a %)	
	2001/02	2009/10		
Pre-school	702,304	1,440,732	738,428	105.1
Primary	2,586,434	3,809,258	1,222,824	47.3
Lower secondary	865,636	1,301,940	436,304	50.4
Upper secondary	328,426[a]	537,332	208,906	63.6
Tertiary	92,530[a]	167,346[b]	74,816	80.9
Total	4,575,330	7,256,608	2,681,278	58.6

Source Calculations based on EMIS data
Note [a]Enrolment figures reflect 2003/04 data
[b]Enrolment figures reflect 2008/09 data

financial resource allocations to the sector. On the same token, young people constitute the vast majority of the entire population in Ghana, with nearly two-thirds (59 %) being 24 years old or younger in 2008 (ibid.). Yet, when a large share of the population is young in the country, both the current and future income generation of the economically active population is very small in relation to the demand for education resources. That is, due to the country's age structure, the labour force (especially the tax-paying labour force) is relatively small and thus the fiscal burden falls on a smaller share of the population. This reinforcing synergy may also help to explain why opening access especially at post-basic levels can be fiscally difficult. If the 15–19-year-old population, accounting for about one in every ten Ghanaians, would be in school, the 2-fold strain on the economically active population would be intensified. First, the size of the labour force and therefore the tax revenue base would decrease even more and, second, additional public funding would be needed to compensate for the large enrolment influxes.

Twenty seven percent of the entire population in Ghana is enrolled in basic education. An increased influx of about 2.7 million children and youth into the school system between 2001/02 and 2009/10 reflects an enormous achievement for the government but also a burden for the education system (Table 7.1). Alone within the academic year 2008/09-2009/10, about 300,000 additional children and youth were absorbed into the sector. In 2009/10, around 6.6 million pupils were studying at the basic education level in Ghana. If all out-of-school children of basic education age were incorporated into the school system, then about one in every three Ghanaians would attend a basic school. Estimates of population data merged with EMIS data show that over the 6-year period 2008/09-2014/15 school-age population groups in Ghana will grow rapidly, with the primary age population likely increasing by about 8.9 %, lower secondary by about 13.2 % and upper secondary by about 14.3 %.

Household Structure: The Number, Age and Gender of Children

At the macro-level, the share of public investment in education is strongly influenced by demography, e.g. how fast the population and therefore new enrolments

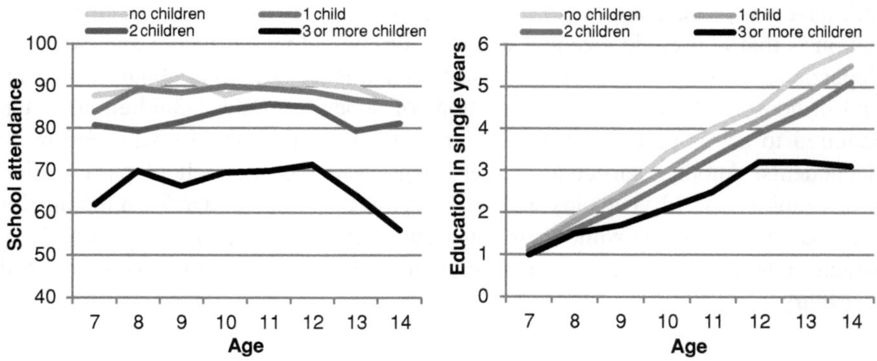

Fig. 7.1 School attendance rates and years of completed education for children by age and the number of household members 5 years of age or younger, 2008/09
Source Author's illustration based on GDHS data calculations
Note The survey sample covers 10,126 children aged 7–14. 6-year olds are not included given a limited number of observations. The share of the 7–14-year-old population with no children 5 or younger living at home accounts for 43.1 % of this population, while 31.9 % have one household member falling into this age group, 17.2 % have 2 children of this age at home and the remaining 7.8 % have three or more children 5 or under living in the same household

grow and what share of the population is of school-age. At the micro-level, a household's investment in education is also largely determined by the number and age of its members. Lower demographic growth rates have therefore just as many positive effects on the country's development as having fewer children has on the prospects of a household, with more and/or longer investments possible in the education of each individual child.

The number of children in a household is a good predictor of whether a child attends school and the highest class which he or she may complete. If a child aged 7–14 lives in a household with more than three children 5 years of age or younger (generally siblings), his or her chances of attending school is 66.4 % compared to 81.9 % for those who live with two children 5 or under at home and 89.1 % for those without any younger children of this age at home (2008/09 GDHS data calculations). Households with a larger number of children competing over limited household resources may see themselves confronted with the trade-off between quantity and quality, so that some or all children may have fewer educational opportunities due to the financial expenses for every additional child. For some the decision to have fewer children can be to maximise on their educational opportunities.

In relation to the number of young siblings at home, school exclusion rises with age. Data analysis conducted in Fig. 7.1 reveals that if households without any children 5 or under constituted their own country, nearly all 14-year olds in these households would have completed primary education (5.9 years of schooling on average) while those with three or more children of this age living at home would still have a very long way to go (an average of 3.1 years of schooling). One explanation is that household size and composition, including the nature and extent of dependency among household members, can impact decisions about schooling, and in households with larger proportions of dependents older children are often required to act as carers and in rural areas work on the farm to help feed more dependents. Another particularly interesting finding is that school participation drops rapidly for 12-year olds with at least three siblings under-5 competing for their parents' resources while their completion rates even become static (Fig. 7.1), which underscores the difficulties in escaping poverty traps, both educational and monetary.

Gender

Educational inequalities between males and females are small in terms of attendance, at least at lower educational levels, while they remain large in terms of completion, especially at higher educational levels. One success story in Ghana is that the gender gap in accessing basic schooling has almost fully closed. Gender parity in school enrolment has nearly been reached in kindergarten (0.99) and primary school (0.96), while it has improved in lower and upper secondary to 0.92 and 0.80, respectively (EMIS 2008/09). The basic education sector has therefore begun to lay the foundation for reducing gender disparities at higher levels of education as well as other forms of gender inequalities in society. The degree to which the government is able to close the current gender gap of about two males for every female enrolled in tertiary institutions will help to determine the rate at which the gender gap in economic opportunities across the country reduces, with women accounting for less than one-third of those employed in the non-agricultural sector in 2008 based on World Development data. Table 7.2 provides evidence of gradual gender convergence in educational attainment especially among upper secondary and tertiary graduates.

Table 7.2 Gender differences in level of education completed by different age groups, 2008/09

	Highest level of education completed							
	For 15–49-year olds				For 20–29-year olds			
	Total	Female	Male	Number of obs.	Total	Female	Male	Number of obs.
No schooling	36.0	41.9	29.1	7,618	30.8	36.8	23.3	2,193
Primary	17.2	17.3	17.1	3,634	12.2	12.0	12.4	869
Lower secondary	30.1	28.2	32.2	6,373	31.1	30.5	32.0	2,214
Upper secondary	15.2	11.7	19.4	3,225	24.7	19.8	30.8	1,754
Tertiary	1.5	0.9	2.2	316	1.2	0.9	1.5	85
Total	100	100	100	21,166	100	100	100	7,115

Source Author's calculations based on GDHS data

Internal and External Migration Patterns

Internal migration mainly takes place among the lesser educated. Calculations from GLSS 2005/06 illustrate that about half of all households (46 %) have one or more migrants. Four-fifths (81 %) remain in the country, of whom over two-thirds (69 %) migrate to urban centres. The Greater Accra and Ashanti regions are the destination of about 56 % of internal migrants. A consequence of these migrant flows is that basic infrastructure and the delivery of social services like education and health are likely to be placed under additional strain in these urban areas, compounded by natural population growth. Contrary to contemporary belief, only one in every ten migrants stem from one of the three northern regions. Migrants are 5 years younger and have less education than the average Ghanaian, with for example 34 % of non-migrants having completed secondary school but only 8 % of migrants. This relationship is not unexpected because 75 % of Ghanaian migrants stem from rural areas where schooling opportunities are more limited. It is important to note that after finding work, education is the second most commonly cited motivation for migration (16.5 % of all migrants).

About one-third of Ghanaians with tertiary education emigrate. Present emigration trends have a substantial brain drain component that affects the labour market, since 22 % of Ghanaians have upper secondary education, but 75 % of those do who emigrate to OECD countries, and 2.2 % of Ghanaians have higher education while 14 % of those who emigrate to such countries do (ibid.). OECD estimates for 2008 suggest that about 35 % of tertiary graduates emigrate from Ghana (World Development data).

About 9 % of total public education spending is 'lost' due to Ghanaians who later emigrate. Compounded with large levels of human capital flight, there is not only a loss of government returns on tertiary subsidies but also a loss of future income tax generation. 82.8 % of international migrants completed their education while living in Ghana. A study by the World Bank (2009a) crosses individuals' migration patterns and levels of education (also using 2005/06 GLSS data) with the unit costs of government expenditure for each level of education (administrative EMIS data). It finds that total education spending for all Ghanaians, whether they emigrated or are still residents in the county, is estimated at 49,116 billion cedis (US$5 billion) using 2004 unit costs, whereas education expenditure for Ghanaians who later emigrated totalled about 4,312 billion cedis (almost US$0.5 billion). This implies that public education expenditure for outbound migrants accounted for about 9 % of total government spending on education.

It is questionable if current levels of remittances are enough to offset the emigration of skills and the public spending leakage. As reported by the Central Bank of Ghana, overall private remittances accounted for about US$1.7 billion in 2008. Remittance inflows provided by national authorities, which include other types of current transfers, trade transactions and informal transfers, are often very high compared to IMF calculations which estimate remittances at US$126 million for 2008—below one-tenth of administrative figures (World Bank 2010a; Joseph and Plaza 2010). IMF estimates suggest therefore that migrant remittances received as a share of GDP total less than 1 %. Moreover, remittances may not always promote pro-poor development. 89 % of emigrants have either upper secondary or tertiary education and 77.4 % of upper secondary graduates and 90.1 % of tertiary graduates come from the top two quintiles (Table 6.1), making the vast majority of the beneficiaries of remittance income likely affluent families.

Interconnections Between Household Demographics and Educational Exclusion

An interesting finding in Table 7.3 is that 17.8 % of children 6–14 years of age who live with a male household head did not attend school compared to only 10.1 % of children living with a female household head. With the vast majority of female household heads being mothers, this supports the notion that mothers may place a greater significance on their children's schooling towards which they may be more inclined to invest additional resources, whether time or money. Another interesting finding is the severity of poverty traps in the North: it is here where about half of 6–14-year olds (46.5 %) do not attend school if there are three or more household members 5 years of age or younger at home compared to 17.5 % in the South.

The overall influence of key individual, household and community variables on school participation is strongest at initial enrolment. An age-profile analysis reveals a number of very interesting findings when disaggregated by disadvantaged and advantaged groups (Fig. 7.2). First, the largest disparities in school participation among different key deprived and privileged groups are observed at the age of six and remain significant for the entire basic school-age population. Second, it appears that irrespective of these background characteristics children gradually begin to leave school at the age of 12 to generally enter the work force (even those in the South and in the richest quintile) and increasingly at the age of 16 and beyond. These two findings appear to support the need for programmes aimed at widening educational opportunities to particularly target the youngest children (6-year olds) while those aimed at reducing dropout to particularly target adolescents 12 years of age and older. Third, among the four (dis-)advantaged groups, disparities for the population aged 17 and older are the largest in relation to gender, while disparities for the population aged 6–16 are the smallest in relation to gender. This helps to illustrate the effectiveness of the government's gender policies in terms of basic school access but simultaneously provides evidence of the need to improve gender quotas in higher classes. Fourth, Northerners experience overall the least opportunities in attending school, given that in this part of the country 12-year olds are the most likely to be schooling but 23 % of them remain at the margin of the school system while this share is lower for all other deprived groups.

By measuring the degree of marginalisation, Fig. 7.3 permits the illustration of multiple drivers of educational inclusion and exclusion simultaneously for 6–14-year olds and of educational vulnerability and privilege simultaneously for 15–19-year olds. It provides further evidence that a wide range of factors—from geography and health to economics and demographics—have self-reinforcing

Table 7.3 Share of children aged 6–14 who did not attend school in the academic year 2008/09, by demographic indicators and (dis-)advantaged groups

All shares refer to school non-attendance rates out of 100 %	Total	North	South	Rural	Urban	Poorest quintile	Richest quintile	Girl	Boy	Total obs.
Total	15.6	28.4	9.3	18.9	9.6	29.4	7.5	15.2	15.9	11,589
Girl	15.2	27.5	9.7	18.0	10.6	29.1	9.4	–	–	5,668
Boy	15.9	29.1	8.9	19.6	8.6	29.6	5.2	–	–	5,921
0 household members aged 5 and under	12.0	21.3	9.0	14.0	9.3	22.8	9.2	11.8	12.2	4,881
1 household member aged 5 and under	13.6	25.0	7.8	16.6	8.2	26.5	4.3	13.0	14.2	3,779
2 household members aged 5 and under	19.9	32.3	11.7	23.0	10.5	32.3	7.7	20.3	19.6	2,023
3 or more household members aged 5 and under	33.7	46.5	17.5	36.2	22.5	44.6	0.0	31.5	35.8	906
Female household head	10.1	18.3	8.3	12.2	7.6	21.6	7.0	10.2	10.0	3,298
Male household head	17.8	30.2	9.9	21.0	10.8	30.8	7.6	17.5	18.1	8,291
Mother not alive, father alive	17.5	27.2	11.7	21.3	9.9	31.6	10.3	19.1	15.4	274
Father not alive, mother alive	16.8	26.9	9.9	20.4	10.2	31.7	8.8	17.6	16.1	701

Source Author's calculations based on GDHS data.

Note School attendance data that refers to children in the richest quintile with three or more household members 5 years of age or younger at home should be read with caution given the limited number of observations

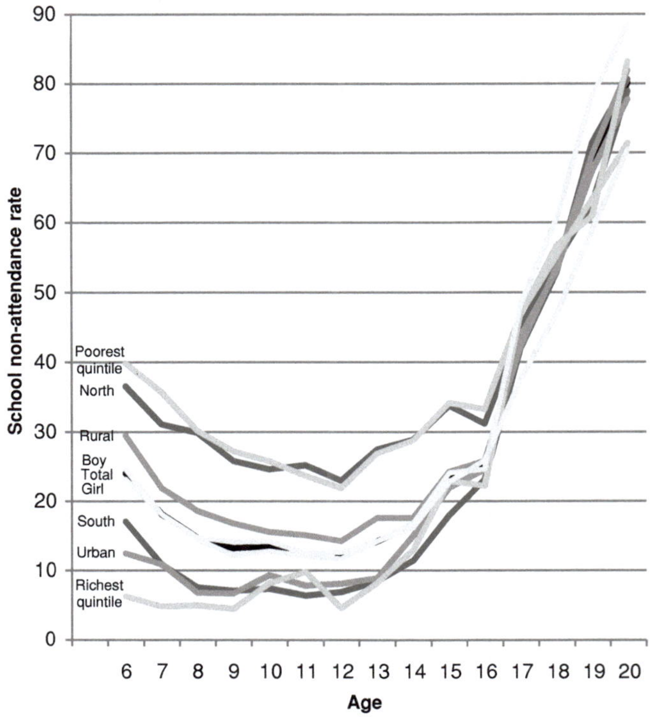

Fig. 7.2 An age-profile of the share of children and youth who did not attend school in the academic year 2008/09, by (dis-)advantaged groups.
Source Author's illustration based on GDHS data calculations

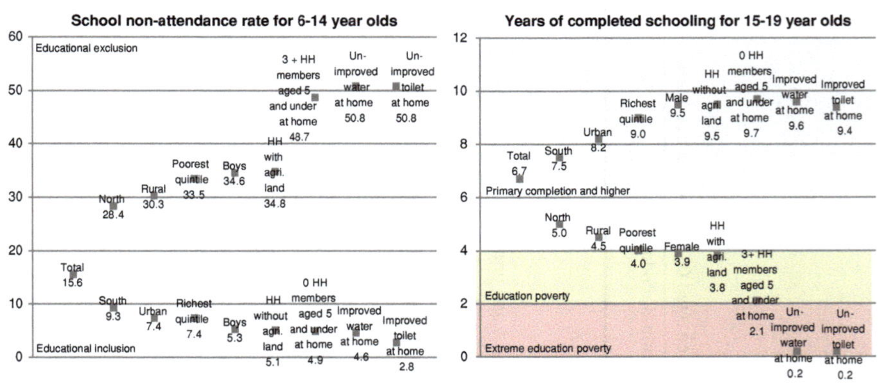

Fig. 7.3 Educational inclusion and exclusion for 6–14-year olds and educational poverty and privilege for 15–19-year olds by combining key background traits, 2008/09.
Source Author's illustration based on GDHS data calculations. *Note* HH stands for household. The survey sample covers 11,589 children 6-14 years of age and 4,842 youth 15–19 years of age. Data does not allow for further disaggregation given the decreasing number of observations. Information on child labour is not collected by GDHS but it is partly captured by households owning land used for agriculture given that nearly all child labourers in Ghana (93.7 %) are employed in non-paid agriculture based on GLSS 2005/06 data

effects on the extent to which an individual is educationally disadvantaged or advantaged in Ghana. While nationally almost one in every six basic school-age children (15.6 %) remain outside of the school system, 'typical' Ghanaian children who have the least opportunities in attending school live in the rural North (attendance rate of 69.7 %) and if they are also males in the poorest quintile within a household owning land used for agriculture their school participation rate decreases to 65.2 % and finally falls to 49.2 % for those who simultaneously have three or more household members aged 5 and under at home and use an unimproved toilet and drinking water source at home (Fig. 7.3). This is an alarming finding because children with these multiple interlocking risk factors that induce extreme education deprivation account for significant shares of children in the country, as for example 10.4 % of all 6–14-year olds are simultaneously males in the poorest quintile within a household owning land used for agriculture in the rural North. The findings of this data analysis imply that the specific background traits (and therefore policy priorities) change as the group of the most educationally marginalised becomes smaller and much more difficult to reach.

Conclusion and Policy Implications: Demographic Patterns and Pressures

Past, current and future population growth is very high and puts significant pressure on the education sector. High demographic growth—from 5 million people in 1950 to 24.3 million by 2010 and projected at 45.2 million for 2050—will continue to retard the country's educational development through (1) persistent influxes of (probably unabsorbable) new school enrolments at all levels, (2) constantly increasing fiscal pressures and (3) very large supply demands on education personnel, infrastructure and services. Almost two-thirds of the entire population is 24 years of age or younger. 27 % of the total population in Ghana is already enrolled in basic education in 2009/10, with over one million children falling into this age group (6–14-year olds) still out of school today and with estimates indicating that this age group will grow by millions in the coming decades who will all require schooling. Population growth has therefore been identified as one of the most important external influences shaping the educational landscape in Ghana. Population growth, together with economic growth, are the two factors that appear to also have the strongest effects on the development of the education sector in other countries such as Malawi (World Bank 2004). The findings above suggest that, because national fertility declined from 6.4 children per woman in 1988 to 4.0 children per woman in 2008 largely due to improved educational attainment (see regression analysis in Chap. 5), parents will be able to invest more into the education of fewer children and thus schooling opportunities will likely continue to widen for Ghanaians and in turn fertility will likely continue to decline. One conclusion is therefore that by improving policy levers to advance equitable education in the country—especially among females in the North given higher fertility levels—this intrinsic dual synergy will be catalysed and further declines in population growth will likely take place.

The number, age and gender of children in a household help shape their schooling status. Households with many young children must bear an increased cost burden and are often restrained from educating all children to the same level, with for example 14-year olds without any siblings aged 5 or under at home having completed an average of 5.9 years of schooling compared to only 3.1 years of schooling among those with three or more young children of this age at home. The odds of dropping out of school, especially for those with many younger siblings, increase with age and completion rates even become stagnant for older children with at least three siblings 5 years of age or younger likely because of the need for additional assistance and childcare at home (Fig. 7.1). Findings also show that the influence of key personal, household and community variables on constraining school participation is strongest at initial enrolment (Fig. 7.2). It will be therefore crucial for respective policies and programmes aimed at widening educational opportunities to place a particular focus on the 6-year-old population, which is both the most marginalised group as well as the most critical group given the adverse effects of being overage in school. In terms of gender, the enrolment gap has nearly closed between girls and boys, at least at the basic education level. At higher levels gender inequalities in both access and outcomes are still large.

Ghana is a country with large levels of brain drain migration. Migratory flows among Ghanaians, whether internal or abroad, are (as expected) often a consequence of imbalances in development between origin and destination areas. Data analysis indicates that one's decision in favour of internal migration is principally based on differences in job and education opportunities largely between disadvantaged areas and urban areas, with those who migrate internally generally being less educated and skilled and seeking better opportunities (2005/06 GLSS data). In contrast to most internal migrants, emigrants are highly educated and skilled, with about one-third of Ghanaians with tertiary education migrating abroad. A challenge facing the government as a result of emigration is losing not only a significant share of the best human capital in the country but also about one-tenth of total education spending as well as subsequent income tax generation, although it is arguable that this triple-strain may more or less be offset by remittance inflows. To reduce negative effects of internal migration that push people out of their communities, one can conclude here that there is a strong necessity to reduce geographic disparities in the country by improving education, skills and labour prospects for those in isolated and disadvantaged areas. To reduce negative effects of emigration and levels of brain drain, it is commonly known that one innovative and successful policy within Ghana's health sector has been that the government requires nurses to verify that they have worked within the country for 5 years after completing their education, before they receive their formal degree. It may be interesting for education planners to analyse the appropriateness of possibly applying such a policy instrument to various university degrees. Policy options are discussed in the following chapter.

Part III
Policy Discussion and Conclusion

Chapter 8
Policy Discussion: Outlining Policy Options and Solutions

In response to the question—*to what extent do you think that data guides policy?*—the Minister of Education indicated during the interview that "we are moving from research into development programmes. You need a lot of data to be able to plan development—on all fronts. [...] So, it is a necessary factor that research must guide". Direct policy dialogue participation in 2010 revealed that this view is in line with those of other senior government officials in Ghana, such as the Deputy Minister of Education, who highlights the necessity for "research findings to have policy relevance for service delivery".[1] Addressing this issue is the central aim of this chapter, while it shows that many of the current policies and programmes are not driven by data analysis.

While the analysis throughout the preceding chapters examines the latest data available and establishes a number of key evolving challenges facing educational planners and stakeholders in opening access and ensuring completion for Ghanaians at different levels of education, this is only the first step. The second step in helping policy-makers make informed decisions is to identify and map out policy options to tackle these challenges. Building on the findings throughout the entire study, this chapter therefore seeks answers to the core question of what combinations of policies and programmes are likely to lead to the greatest access and attainment in Ghana especially for educationally deprived groups in years to come.

Limited education is a solvable challenge that requires effective policy action. In the following, a more incisive look is taken at the specific actions needed, whether reforming existing policies, making programmes more efficient, developing new interventions or building up capacities, to contribute to greater educational access and attainment for Ghanaians. Findings revealed that influences at both the micro-level (individual, household, community and regional) and macro-level (national) have strong effects on levels of education in the country, with the former largely reliant on the latter. This relationship has been outlined in the conceptual framework (Fig. 1.1) and established via analysis findings. While policies to promote education and skills development will likely need to address issues at both levels, findings in the analysis suggest that education policy itself may generally

[1] This particular quote from the Deputy Minister of Education is from technical discussions in the Ministry of Education on the 29th–30th of September, 2010 between senior government officials, development partners and university professors. The author participated in collaboration with the World Bank.

A. Krauss, *External Influences and the Educational Landscape*,
SpringerBriefs in Economics, DOI: 10.1007/978-1-4614-4936-2_8,

have the greatest observable effects on the wide range of contributing factors at the individual, family, community and regional level (relative to the macro-level).

There are at least three reasons for reducing the broad array of external factors with varying levels of effects on the education sector to a smaller number of key factors. First, not all factors are directly relevant for policy. For example, policies that would be targeted along religious and/or ethnic lines would be accompanied by high implementation costs and social stigma. Second, the factors with the greatest need should receive the greatest resource attention given the country's constrained fiscal environment. For example, it is established that some variables have fewer effects on the education sector in Ghana than in other sub-Saharan countries (e.g. HIV/AIDS, gender disparities in access at lower levels) and therefore should be allocated relatively lower levels of resources. Third, from a policy and managerial perspective, ensuring that every issue affecting school-age children somewhere in the country is reflected in policy planning would overstretch the country's already strained institutional capacity. Before proceeding, it is necessary to discuss critical target groups of policies and programmes.

The forces driving educational marginalisation, socioeconomic deprivation and geographic isolation are highly interconnected. Map 8.1 crosses data for 6–14-year olds who are attending school with the respective average welfare quintile of the households in which they live and illustrates this data spatially across the country. It does the same for 15–19-year olds who have finished the primary cycle and for 17–19-year olds who are basic school graduates. This needs assessment provides further evidence that the three Northern regions are consistently the most educationally and socioeconomically deprived areas of the country. The gap in attendance rates of 6–14-year olds is 19 % between the North (71.7 %) and the South (90.7 %), while the gap in primary completion for 15–19-year olds is 26.8 % (53.2 to 80.0 %) and the gap in lower secondary completion for 17–19-year olds is 29 % (23.8 to 52.8 %). Statistical analysis beyond the basic school level indicates that the North continues to be incrementally more disadvantaged at the upper secondary and tertiary levels in terms of both access and attainment (data not shown in map). Given that education indicators are closely linked to geographic location and welfare levels at home (as regression results in Table 6.6 also verify), it appears that households have the desire to ensure their children go to and complete school provided that opportunity costs of schooling in specific communities are low and household resources allow for it.

It is of fundamental importance for different policy levers to target Northerners. The findings here—together with the data-driven analysis throughout the study that illustrates the largest disparities on a number of education indicators between the North and the South (overall larger than those for different welfare levels, gender and other factors)—have implications on policy in terms of programme targeting. Geographic maps, for example of gaps in primary or basic school completion, of income poverty or of food insecurity, are commonly used to determine potential beneficiaries of targeted government interventions (see e.g. World Bank 2010e). Map 8.1 provides evidence that geographic targeting of the North on a range of policies and programmes discussed below may be a viable policy solution, while there is likely political pressure to continue implementing some educational programmes on a national scale. There are at least four reasons in favour of North targeting for a number of already existing and new interventions: (1) it would reach the most educationally deprived at all levels as

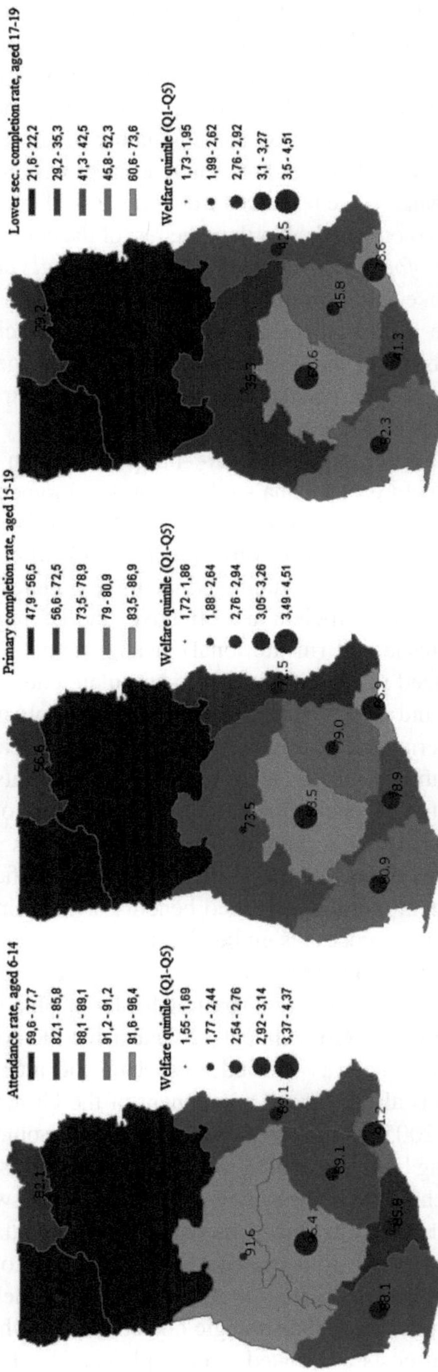

Map 8.1 Targeting the educationally and socioeconomically deprived North: share of school attendees aged 6–14, primary graduates aged 15–19 and basic school graduates aged 17–19 and their welfare levels at home, 2008/09

Source Author's illustration based on GDHS data calculations

Note This survey sample covers 11,589 children 6–14 years of age, 4,842 youth 15–19 years of age and 2,812 youth 17–19 years of age well as the most socioeconomically disadvantaged; (2) it is very likely to be a more efficient and effective approach at universalising education compared to implementing various universal programmes and safety nets or compared to targeting specific groups within all areas of the country (see also World Bank 2010e); (3) it would therefore likely not only reduce administrative costs but also require less implementation capacity at the local level and is less likely to cause any stigma (as all are recipients within a given area); and (4) it is very likely to lead to a more even provision of educational goods and services across Ghana, while resources would run less of a risk of being dissipated and they would help to connect the North to the rest of the country.

A results- and capacity-focused roadmap for educational development is needed. It is important to take into account that financial resources by themselves will neither be able nor be needed to tackle many challenges facing the sector. Rather, improving the capability of the government to better manage policies, systems, processes and results will be needed to address many constraints. The traditional investment approach in the education sector—with nearly all budgetary allocations and interventions being supply-driven—has proven often inefficient and ineffective at the current juncture of Ghana's education development, as the analysis has shown. It is argued here that in an environment of evolving educational needs like in Ghana, most improvements towards greater levels of equitable education will be made by (1) continually fine-tuning educational policies to make them better targeted, and more relevant, efficient and effective, and (2) regularly reviewing and strengthening organisational (institutional) arrangements. Policy planners and makers will therefore need to identify means to stimulate educational demand and enhance the efficiency and effectiveness of educational supply, while building up the government's managerial and institutional capability for educational change.

Building on the findings throughout the analysis, Table 8.1 presents a results- and capacity-focused policy matrix. To help facilitate policy prioritisation in a country with limited resources and capacity, a unique feature of the matrix is the creation of a column for the estimated financial and political costs of specific interventions towards the goal's achievement and the estimated benefits of these interventions. It ensures that the policy planning process is embedded in a focused goal which is to increase educational access and outcomes for Ghanaians at all levels, but particularly to attain free, compulsory and universal basic education. This is not only the most fundamental objective of the Government of Ghana for the education sector (Ministry of Education 2009) and was verified as such in the interview with the Minister of Education but it is also a central component of the Growth and Poverty Reduction Strategy (NDPC 2005). Steps towards its attainment would, as the statistical analysis illustrated, bring both large social and economic benefits to Ghanaians. To help achieve this overarching goal, the policy matrix aims to answer the following five questions: (1) which strategic objectives will support the attainment of the goal, (2) which binding constraints (to a strategic objective) need to be addressed, (3) which interventions, including policy tools, programmes, deliverables and resource inputs, are needed to achieve the strategic objectives, (4) what are the estimated financial and political costs associated with implementing the interventions and their estimated benefits and (5) what expected outcomes (of the interventions) are needed to achieve the strategic objectives and advance the goal?

Table 8.1 Results- and capacity-focused policy matrix to increase educational access and outcomes at all levels in Ghana

Binding constraint	Policy, programme or reform approach	Financial cost ($) political cost (*) benefit (+)	Expected outcome
Strategic objective: Integrate the remaining out-of-school children and increase attendance at the basic education level with a focus on the geographically disadvantaged and child labourers			
A lack of suitable flexibility and of resistance to corruption of a policy instrument The capitation grant has been a key policy in stimulating enrolment growth (between 2004/05–2007/08 as the country reached historical highs) and, if reformed, could become a key enrolment-driver once again. Its target population needs to be reformed and minimised, while the grant is also plagued with resource leakage and misappropriation (CDD 2010)—reforming the capitation grant is discussed in detail later in the chapter	• Improve targeting of the capitation grant by transferring funds to the North (instead of nationwide allocations) and possibly to households (instead of schools) so that the most disadvantaged become the principal beneficiaries	$/**/+++ No extra funding would be needed as grant allocations would simply be redistributed but some political opposition could arise in reforming this high-profile policy in the country	Such a reformed grant would, if current levels of investment remain constant, increase the annual grant funding per capita in the North, which at GH¢4.50 currently only accounts for 8.5 percent of annual household costs per primary student at GH¢52.81, to reflect an average of 44.8 % of household expenses per Northern primary student (2005/06 GLSS data calculations), as 19 % of the total primary-age population lives in the North. It would improve the grant's impact and efficiency and reduce levels of resource leakage
	• Ensure consistent school visits are conducted by circuit supervisors and/or independent evaluators to audit grant transfers more closely and ensure school authorities *de facto* abolish school fees for at least grant sponsored activities	$/*/+ Minimal additional costs would be linked to this measure	
Low school demand due to weak compatibility with community norms and resource-constrained households The statistical analysis found that one of the factors explaining why one in every six children 6–14 years of age did not attend school in the academic year 2008/09 (GDHS) is because of the resource constraints of households which affect their ability to afford fees for children's school tuition, lunch, uniforms, learning materials etc. (Chap. 6)	• Better supervise and consistently audit school authorities to ensure they truly abolish all forms of direct user fees for basic education as already laid out by the government in the fcuBE policy (Ministry of Education 2009)	$$$/*/+++ Political consensus on the fcuBE policy but also the free school uniforms- and learning materials- policy exists as they have already been legally adopted, but they will require additional funding (particularly fcuBE) to ensure that they are 'fully' implemented and done so in a sustainable way	Even if improved oversight mechanisms and implementation of these respective policy instruments are not able to get rid of all direct costs for schooling, they would nonetheless help to decrease the large financial burden of schooling falling on many vulnerable households and help to incentivise their children's schooling

(continued)

Table 8.1 (continued)

Binding constraint	Policy, programme or reform approach	Financial cost ($) political cost (*) benefit (+)	Expected outcome
Strategic objective: Integrate the remaining out-of-school children and increase attendance at the basic education level with a focus on the geographically disadvantaged and child labourers			
Low school demand due to weak compatibility with community norms and child labour needs, and a lack of suitable flexibility of a policy instrument One in six children aged 6-14 are involved in child labour. The removal of school fees is often not enough to attract children. Initiated in 2008, LEAP (Livelihood Empowerment Against Poverty) is a cash transfer programme—conditional on school attendance, health visits and no child labour involvement—that is aimed at positively discriminating families in the lowest quintile among the poor with income substitution. Grant amounts are determined by the number of household dependents, ranging from GH¢8-15 monthly (US$5.20-10.30 at 2010 exchange rates) World Bank 2010e)	• Consider simplifying the targeting mechanism of the LEAP policy by scaling up its focus and scope on the North	$/*/+++ As administrative costs account for nearly half of total programme expenses, targeting LEAP to the North could almost double the number of total beneficiaries (currently 32,000 households in 2010) without requiring extra financing (see also World Bank 2010e)	LEAP is already regarded as a key policy to attract the most marginalised children into school (ibid.). At the same time however, such a reformed LEAP policy would not only significantly reduce administrative costs but it would also promote extreme poverty reduction in the most disadvantaged part of the country. It would also help to reduce indirect costs, offset opportunity costs and raise demand for schooling, all of which are necessary if child labour is to be overcome and basic education is to be truly free and universal
Low school demand due to weak compatibility with community norms and child labour needs, and a lack of adaptability of organisational arrangements Child labour is more pervasive in rural areas where school attendance patterns can at times reflect seasonal needs (Awedoba et al. 2003). Policies that do not consider local community demands can inadvertently have negative effects on rural livelihoods insofar as they may oblige some households to choose between either work or schooling (Chap. 6)	• Consider adopting a more flexible school operation schedule in rural areas by shifting the start dates and holiday periods of the school calendar and hours of the actual school day possibly at the district level to reduce conflicts with children's family work on the farm	$/**/++ No extra financing would be needed as the same school costs for the same number of school days would apply but on a different school schedule. Since a previous NDC Government has discussed potentially adapting the school calendar to this end, political interest exists although a revived data-driven discussion would be needed.	A policy of matching the school calendar with the farming calendar would help to bring out-of-school child labourers into the system and decrease seasonal absenteeism among both teachers and pupils given that they would be able to assist during planting and harvesting times (see also Awedoba et al. 2003)

(continued)

Table 8.1 (continued)

Binding constraint	Policy, programme or reform approach	Financial cost ($) political cost (*) benefit (+)	Expected outcome
Strategic objective: Integrate the remaining out-of-school children and increase attendance at the basic education level with a focus on the geographically disadvantaged and child labourers			
	• Scale up the School For Life programme in Northern Ghana and ensure its sustainability, as its schooling schedule accommodates for the child labour needs of households	$/*/++ Minimal funding would be needed as the programme has very low operational costs	
Poor achievement of outcomes due to insufficient physical resources 22.5 % of primary students take at least 1 hour to get to and come home from school (Table 4.3) and there are somewhat fewer primary schools relative to the respective population share in the North compared to the South	• Ensure the provision of sufficient primary school structures (with water and toilet facilities) so that children do not commute more than 3 or 4 kilometres to school—especially required in rural areas	$$$/*/+ Building classrooms is generally very expensive, although it has political support among senior policy makers (evidenced in the interview with the Minister of Education)	This approach would help decrease pressure on existing school infrastructure and reduce the share of crowded and open-air classrooms that are known to negatively affect retention rates (Chap. 4), although school construction has decreasing returns (see also Pritchett 2004)
A lack of adaptability of organisational arrangements Resources are very poorly and inefficiently allocated to the government's so-called 'deprived districts' which account for one-third of all districts and are recipients of disproportionately more public funding. Since its inception a decade ago, the policy architecture—which still classifies 'deprived districts' using 2001 data—needs to undergo reform in order to reflect the current reality in these districts. Statistical analysis using 2008/09 EMIS data reveals that 14 of the 53 'deprived districts' already reached 100 % net enrolment in primary and many others have surpassed the national average primary net enrolment at 88.5 %. Also, the scheme is currently too closely linked to supply-side issues (if schools need repairs, seating places etc.) and needs to better reflect demand-side issues	• Redefine the government's 'deprived districts' scheme using the latest data to better reflect changing educational needs. • Consider reforming the targeting criterion for 'deprived districts' to subsidise the first fifty districts that fall below the national average net primary enrolment of 88.5 % and simultaneously fall into the bottom two quintiles which would positively discriminate the poorest households in the country, both educationally and monetarily	$/*/++ No additional costs are foreseen (for a policy of redistribution) except for potential initial administrative costs, while efforts to help maximise the efficiency of public expenditure will likely have strong political support	This would reduce large levels of misallocation of public spending and channel 'additional' funding to the districts that are truly most deprived

(continued)

Table 8.1 (continued)

Binding constraint	Policy, programme or reform approach	Financial cost ($) political cost (*) benefit (+)	Expected outcome
Strategic objective: Reduce non-enrolment and school absenteeism due to children's health status			
A lack of suitable flexibility and of resistance to corruption of a policy instrument High levels of malnutrition and anaemia in Ghana cause irreversible physical and mental stunting of children. The school feeding programme that helps tackle these challenges is currently poorly administered and very unequally distributed, with 23.1% of primary students covered by the programme in the South and 12.4 % in the North (see chapter 5). It also has a strong poverty-reducing dimension as parents save a very significant share of household income on school meals: 195 school days x 0.30–0.40 pesewas = GH¢58.50-78.00 a year (or US$40-54 at 2010 exchange rates). It is important to remember that while providing school meals especially during the first several years of primary schooling has positive effects on both schooling and health indicators, targeting even younger children is equally necessary as malnutrition can cause stunting and thus can affect late school enrolment (ibid.)	• Reallocate resources of the school feeding programme to the most needy groups by minimising (possibly eliminating) its scope in the South and by targeting the entire North of Ghana, where most hungry, poor and/or out-of-school children live.	$/*/+++ Such spatial resource reallocation would likely require no extra funding, as 20.7 % of all children in primary school in 2008/09 are beneficiaries but only 19 % of the total primary-age population lives in the North (see Chap. 5). At the same time, political support would likely be high as the reform would enhance the programme's targeting efficiency given its objective.	Expanding this vital social safety net in the North via simple geographic targeting would improve the programme's very poor resource allocation, support children of impoverished households, reduce malnutrition and anaemia rates and incentivise parents to ensure their children are in school
	• Consider expanding the programme's target population to include all pre-schoolers (4 to 5 year olds) in the North.	$$$/**/++ Universalising coverage for pre-schoolers in the North would be both financially and politically feasible, given the small population size.	
	• Consider expanding provision of iron supplements as part of the school feeding programme, as most children and youth are anaemic in Ghana (Chap. 5)	$/*/++ Minimal funding would be required as it would be absorbed into the administrative and implementation structure of the school feeding programme	
Poor achievement of outcomes due to sickness, infection and absenteeism as a result of insufficient school infrastructure 33.5 % of primary schools have no access to drinking water and 42 % have no toilets, with much higher shares in the North (EMIS data). Children and youth tend to have lower enrolment and attainment levels in schools where clean water and/or functioning sanitation facilities are lacking (Chap. 5)	• Construct improved water and toilet facilities in all schools, including waste disposal facilities	$$/*/++ Political will exists to universalise these basic amenities in schools, as policy targets have already been adopted by the government (Ministry of Education 2008; Netherlands Development Organisation 2008) but additional funding will still be needed	This would help to reduce dehydration and poor hygiene in schools and decrease the incidence of sickness and infection among children and youth (Chap. 5)

(continued)

Table 8.1 (continued)

Binding constraint	Policy, programme or reform approach	Financial cost ($) political cost (*) benefit (+)	Expected outcome
Strategic objective: Increase opportunities in upper secondary, TVET and higher education and thereby help promote skills development and economic growth			
A lack of adaptability of organisational arrangements There is a severe imbalance in the skills supply for and skills demand of the labour market, with an unfulfilled supply of science and technology graduates and an excess of graduates in arts and humanities (Chap. 3)	• Establish enrolment quotas to achieve the government target of reaching a share of 60 % of university students registered in disciplines related to science and technology by the year 2020 (see Ministry of Education 2010), while the share was 37.7 % in 2007/08 based on EMIS data.	$/*/+++ No or only minimal costs would accompany this measure as it largely involves a shifting of enrolment quotas for respective subjects whereas tuition fees are typically the same across different disciplines. The government has furthermore already endorsed the 60 % target	This would help to increase employment rates among graduates, raise the efficiency and effectiveness of public investment in higher education and promote critical drivers for national development
	• Establish a network to link education/skills supply to its labour market demand by increasing engagement of industry and employers in issues of curriculum content and skill needs	$/*/++ Minimal funding would be needed (for administrative purposes), while political support would likely be strong in improving the relevance of education and the external efficiency of the sector	This would increase involvement of private sector actors to find broad consensus on sectoral needs and educational priorities
A lack of adaptability of organisational arrangements to geographic conditions Distance education, a tool for opening access to schooling especially at higher levels, can help to overcome many barriers to education, notably geographic but also gender and economic barriers. In addition, tertiary institutions do not have the capacity, in terms of facilities and personnel, to take in all qualified candidates (Kwapong 2007)	• Consider the feasibility of expanding open universities (distance learning institutions) and training relevant personnel as a complimentary and cost-effective means to open up tertiary education.	$$/*/++ Additional funding would be needed in terms of human resources but no or only minimal funding in terms of physical resources. Given its cost-efficiency relative to traditional tertiary institutions, political support may exist	This would help to drive increased levels of tertiary education especially among the most geographically disadvantaged and, among other benefits, would help scale up the highly skilled labour force at lower than usual public costs

(continued)

Table 8.1 (continued)

Binding constraint	Policy, programme or reform approach	Financial cost ($) political cost (*) benefit (+)	Expected outcome
	Strategic objective: Free up resources for alternative and additional investments		
Low levels of operational efficiency Financial support is (as mentioned) not required to tackle many of the sectoral constraints identified here. Yet, as a World Bank (2011) study found, there is very much room to reduce inefficiencies in terms of teacher salaries in Ghana. Education spending on teachers accounts for 96 % of education expenditure, or over one quarter of all government spending in 2010 (EMIS data), and large shares of this spending are poorly allocated (ibid.)	• Slim down the share of education spending for teachers by rationalising staff, eliminating ghost teachers (remunerated but absent teachers) and other unutilised personnel (see World Bank 2011) and ensure a more equitable district-level distribution of teachers	$/**/+++ This would likely imply very large gains in levels of available education funding, but since teacher unions are well organised in Ghana (as field research indicates), carrying out such reforms may be politically challenging	Efficiency gains in teacher salaries would very likely be the most feasible and effective strategy to free up large amounts of public resources for education. It would also help reduce the donor funding demands
	Strategic objective: Enhance capacity to achieve greater outcomes		
Low operational efficiency due to weak public management that leads to poor achievement of outcomes A very important finding of direct policy dialogue with the government in 2010 is that many government staff have limited experience in conducting a number of administrative and managerial tasks such as formulating work plans and terms of references, among others. This is a critical component of the relatively low overall capability of the government not only in effectively implementing policies and programmes and continually reforming these, but also (at least as important) in managing everyday tasks in the Ministry (note-taking, following a detailed work plan etc.)	• Conduct training workshops (possibly for 1-2 weeks every year) in public administration and management for mid- and senior-level ministerial staff	$/**/+++ Training workshops can be conducted at very low costs (and are often externally funded), while the degree of high-level political support required to carry out such training would need to be further explored	This would build up the government's managerial skills, implementation know-how and overall capacity by helping to prioritise agendas, to be more results-focused and, among other benefits, to operate more efficiently and effectively. In addition, it would help improve the capability of government staff to better manage policies and programmes, and systems and processes, which is needed to address many of the binding constraints outlined in this table

(continued)

Table 8.1 (continued)

Binding constraint	Policy, programme or reform approach	Financial cost ($) political cost (*) benefit (+)	Expected outcome
	Strategic objective: Enhance capacity to achieve greater outcomes		
Low operational efficiency due to weak data management that leads to poor achievement of outcomes The government as well as development partners and the academia do not collect data on several key indicators in Ghana, without which it will be difficult to fully comprehend the causes and consequences of various phenomena affecting education and therefore to formulate coherent and efficient policies. The basic motto is: if it is not measured, it is not managed and cannot be directly influenced. This refers not only to specific education indicators, but there are also groups in society that are not specifically captured in government or household survey data such as street children. In addition, the government currently has low capability to manage data and results, as field research conducted in 2010 and data analysis above indicate	• Administrative EMIS enrolment indicators need to include age at enrolment for each specific year as current indicators hide the true reality behind enrolment patterns and over-age children.	$/*/+ No extra funding would be required as age-specific enrolment indicators could simply be included into the existing annual school survey.	An improved system of data-collection, analysis and management would have a number of benefits by helping: to identify evolving constraints in the sector, to gain a better understanding of changing needs of vulnerable groups (such as street children), to better plan school calendars possibly reflecting farming seasons, to identify human resource needs for the labour market and thus to improve the relevance of education. It would thereby help policy planners to develop more sound and evidence-based policies and programmes that better cater to the particular needs of children and youth, while also helping to better target existing programmes and thus to enhance the efficiency of overall public expenditure
	• Collect data on street children by possibly including relevant variables in the major national surveys (GLSS, GDHS) and by adapting their data collection mechanisms to also survey non-household units (i.e. independent children).	$/*/++ No or only minimal funding would be required as respective indicators could simply be included into the major national household surveys already conducted.	
	• Conduct data-driven needs assessments of programmes such as in this study possibly on a yearly basis and, as applicable, modify beneficiaries, as the data analysis reveals that most programmes are very poorly targeted (the school feeding programme, deprived districts scheme, capitation grant etc.)	$/*/+++ Likely no financial expenses would fall on the public sector as such assessments (when conducted) would be generally externally financed but large financial savings could be made for the government by improving the targeting efficiency of programmes	

Source The content is derived from the author's analysis findings throughout the study, if not otherwise cited

To provide a more detailed description of the specific binding constraints and detailed diagnosis of the change process needed to achieve outcomes, the methodological structure of the policy matrix has been partly influenced by the Capacity Development Results Framework, which the author helped adapt to another West African country in collaboration with the World Bank in 2011 and which has been amended and expanded for this policy matrix to include other relevant features not captured in the framework, particularly the estimated financial and political costs as well as benefits (for an overview of the framework see: World Bank 2009c). Estimated costs and benefits are classified here as follows: $ No or low cost; $$ moderate cost; $$$ high cost. *Low political cost; **moderate political cost; ***high political cost. +Low benefit; ++moderate benefit; +++high benefit. Political costs are defined here above all as how politically difficult would the implementation of a given reform approach be for the central government. The main agent of change for most discussed policy reforms is the Ministry of Education and/or other ministries with education-related objectives and programmes, with private sector actors at times also contributing to the change process

A few of the reforms and interventions discussed here, although beyond the targeted scope of this study, will require comprehensive costing before policy-makers will be able to set policy priorities. Others will require ongoing assessment of results so that corrective action can be taken. It is argued here that this latter need appears to possibly be the most persistent binding constraint facing the education sector: the low capability of the government to consistently fine-tune and administer policies and programmes to make them better targeted, and more relevant, efficient and effective (for which solutions are outlined in Table 8.1). It goes without saying that, although many of the key policy reforms needed are discussed here, there are other policy responses that could be appropriate in addressing the underlying constraints and therefore the policy matrix is not necessarily exhaustive. Before drawing final conclusions, a brief assessment of the capitation grant is conducted in the following, given that it is seen by many in Ghana, as field research indicates, as the main policy instrument to attract the remaining out-of-school children into the system.

The capitation grant was adopted to help abolish all school fees. The capitation grant scheme was piloted in 2004. By 2005 its scope had been extended nationwide, and in 2011 it continues to provide per capita grants to all kindergarten, primary and junior secondary schools. Its objective is to help offset 'private costs' for schooling by providing public basic schools with resources to help upgrade school infrastructure, including sanitation facilities and furniture, sports equipment and school materials (CDD 2010), making the grant a rather supply-driven policy lever.

The capitation grant needs to tackle resource leakage and misappropriation. In response to the question on the grant's resource leakage, the Minister of Education indicated during the interview that losses of public resources

> are social problems. [...] First of all, the authorities themselves [are] providing School Feeding and Capitation Fund in a way that nobody monitors to see whether those schools targeted to benefit from these things are really benefiting from it. [...] monitoring is very weak. [...] If you go to the meetings, they just get together and buy Fanta [a soft drink] [...] and they put it down in their records [as] in-service training.

With a clear degree of openness and transparency, the Minister admits to cases of corruption related to the capitation grant, while acknowledging the need for improved grant monitoring. Nonetheless, the leakage of public funds is indeed a social problem in Ghana, but in having effects on the grant's effectiveness, the Ministry of Education has a responsibility to enhance the administration of funding disbursements, for which solutions are mapped out inTable 8.1 above.

The capitation grant could be targeted to the North instead of nationally. With education expenses incurred by households being 15.7 times that of the capitation grant at the basic school level, the grant should be based on equity and not equality because its current targeting structure is likely to do nothing in terms of reducing educational disparities between different areas of the country and will rather likely contribute to widening these. Since the government's principal educational objective is to reach universal basic education—i.e. attract and maintain the remaining and most disadvantaged children in the system—it must disproportionately support these children and therefore it is argued here that public resources are very poor allocated with the nationwide policy of the capitation grant.

The capitation grant could be targeted to households instead of schools. By reforming the disbursement arrangements and allocating grant funds directly to households (i.e. reducing levels of transaction and bypassing schools and possibly districts), this may likely make the management of funds more transparent and mitigate corruption and the large shares of resource leakage, especially since the current structure can incentivise schools to report higher than actual enrolments in order to receive more grant funding as it is per capita-based. Even more importantly, with hundreds of thousands of children outside the school system in the North, they do not receive any benefits from the capitation grants as these are transferred to school authorities and not to households. Such a direct voucher scheme would also allow, depending on location, some clients (households) to decide on which school to send their children, in which case it is conceivable that schools could become more performance-based to better attract students. It is important to note that the government does have the institutional capacity to carry out such a reformed scheme proposed here, evidenced by for example conditional cash transfers to households already being applied in the country through the LEAP policy.

Based on the findings throughout the analysis, it is argued that—at the sector's current juncture—non-universal and truly demand-side interventions will be most effective in opening access and improving outcomes at the basic education level. The capitation grant, adopted with high expectations as possibly the main driver towards universal basic schooling, does not fulfil either of these two criteria. Until the capitation grant is reformed to become more demand-driven and pro-North (or until an improved policy is adopted), universal education will likely remain out of reach.

In closing, this policy chapter builds on the challenges and risks identified in the preceding chapters. In addressing the question of which coping strategies need to be adopted with urgency to reach the most underserved, get them into school and keep them in school until they complete higher levels, the chapter maps out a number of possible policy responses and reforms for consideration by policymakers and practitioners. It helps to inform on potential paths to build up administrative and institutional capabilities, to increase the efficiency of public expenditure and the effectiveness of public policies and interventions and thereby to improve the educational landscape in Ghana. The following and final chapter concludes with the key findings, implications and emerging challenges derived from the entire analysis.

Chapter 9
Conclusion: Coping Strategies, Emerging Challenges and Opportunities

Why is it so important to gain a better understanding of the specific sources of educational exclusion in Ghana and to outline a number of reforms needed for its reduction? The answer appears obvious: to allow every child to complete at least the basic cycle of education and thus to improve equitable human and economic development and the living conditions of Ghanaians. However, well over one million children of basic school age are still outside the school system. By exploring political, economic, geographic, health and demographic factors affecting the education sector of today and tomorrow, the main purpose of the analysis has been to identify the conditions and characteristics of these out-of-school children and of educationally disadvantaged youth and young adults, the root causes of their vulnerability and exclusion, and thereby help to inform decision-makers and actors who draft and implement public policy of possible ways to achieve universal education and promote more equitable skills development in Ghana. The analysis provides a first attempt at empirically assessing the effects of individual, household, community, regional and national factors on educational marginalisation and privilege simultaneously, and does this applying the latest data available in Ghana. It is therefore hoped that this study, by taking stock of the underlying risk- and enabling-factors of educational change and thus by determining priority areas for resource mobilisation, makes a contribution on how to best utilise existing and new resources and catalyse efforts towards increased educational opportunities and outcomes in the country.

Given that reviews of the central findings are provided at the end of each chapter, the objective of this closing chapter is threefold: first, the main research questions that were laid out in the introduction and guide the entire analysis are returned to in a summarised fashion and the interconnections between these questions are outlined; second, coping strategies for policy to improve the educational landscape are derived from the main findings, and; finally, emerging challenges and opportunities are mapped out.

A. Krauss, *External Influences and the Educational Landscape*,
SpringerBriefs in Economics, DOI: 10.1007/978-1-4614-4936-2_9

Addressing the Main Research Questions

- How and to what extent do political, economic, geographic, health and demographic factors affect educational access and attainment in Ghana?

While much research exists on what happens inside the classroom in affecting the schooling experience of children and youth, much less exists on what happens outside the classroom in influencing access to, progression through or completion of different educational cycles. By turning the focus to the wide-range of external factors at both the macro and micro levels, the analysis attempts to help fill this research gap by assessing the Ghanaian context and argues that the combination of outside influences can determine the performance of the sector more so than school-specific factors, and therefore need to be much better reflected in policy formulation and programmes.

The underlying causes of non-attendance and low educational attainment can be complexly interdependent, multifaceted and cross-sectoral. They can vary from factors as wide-spread in their influence as political instability, slow economic growth and persistent population pressure to those as specific in their manifestation as the geographic isolation of particular groups, the demographic make-up at home and the health, labour and migration status of individual children, youth and adults, as outlined in the conceptual framework in Fig. 1.1 that helped guide the empirical analysis.

Educational development in Ghana is influenced most by demographic pressure and economic growth followed by the North–South divide. Findings show that of a number of external factors at the macro and micro levels influencing educational development, it is possible to discern among the most important influencers at the national level (macroeconomic and demographic environment), at the regional level (the geographic divide between the North and South) and at the individual, household and community level (labour and nutritional status).

Three factors are at the forefront. First, continued high demographic growth (four children per woman in 2008) strongly retards the country's educational development through persistent influxes of (likely unabsorbable) new school enrolments at all levels, through very large supply demands on education personnel, infrastructure and services, and through substantial and incremental fiscal pressures. Estimates indicate that the basic school age population alone will grow by millions in the coming decades who will all require schooling (including the over one million children still out of school today) (Chap. 7). Second, the magnitude, structure and growth of the Ghanaian economy determine almost entirely the amount of public spending and resources available for the education sector and the degree to which these fluctuate. Over the period 2000–2008, annual economic growth at 5.3 % surpassed all historical highs and consequently so did public spending on education at 8 % of GDP, while taking into account that funding—although a vital prerequisite—will by no means be enough to bring educational change alone (Chap. 3). Together, economic and demographic growth strongly shape the constraining and enabling environment for educational development at the individual, household, community and regional level. Third, birth place in the North or South is one of the strongest predictors of an individual's future human capital in Ghana. If the South constituted its own country, nearly every 17-year-old would have already attained primary completion for example, while if the North formed its own country, almost one quarter of youth of this age would not have had this chance. The isolation and marginalisation of the North is caused mainly by the high opportunity costs of schooling as most livelihoods are in subsistence farming in this part of the country, and by its past political neglect and continued limited political attention reflected in lower levels of allocated resources (funding, teachers and physical facilities). Regression analysis shows that geographic location in the North has the largest explanatory value—even larger than variables like welfare quintile levels—in constraining school participation and also determining labour participation among control variables at the child, parent, household, regional and cluster level (Table 6.6). Given these findings, the analysis breaks away from the conventional thinking that monetary poverty largely explains educational poverty and stresses the point that being born in the North can often cause educational and monetary poverty (with the North home to all districts that fall into the bottom quintile), while educational and monetary poverty does not cause relocation to the North (Chap. 4).

Improving equitable levels of education in Ghana in coming years will continue to largely rely on how rapidly current high population growth reduces (and the influx of potential recipients of education services), how rapidly the economy continues to grow (and levels of available education expenditure) and how rapidly the disparity between the North and South reduces (and inequitable resource distribution and high opportunity costs of schooling). While these three influences have been identified as the most important in affecting the country's educational development, findings emerging from the analysis show that addressing—in parallel—a number of issues at the individual, household and community level will be of fundamental importance, particularly child labour and malnutrition/anaemia.

The main explanation for the very large North–South educational gap is that a number of health, economic and demographic factors often come together to disadvantage Northerners. In terms of child labour, the fact that the majority of out-of-school children of basic school age in the North are engaged in labour activities, makes child labour the leading alternative to schooling (Chap. 6). Nearly all of the about 317,000 child labourers 6–14 years of age are involved in farming activities and the country's strong agricultural dependency also contributes to lower demand for education as well as a volatile and more limited public resource pool to fund education policies and programmes (Chap. 3). Given that child labour is separate from the decision to attend school for almost one in every ten children 6–14 years old in the country, opening up educational opportunities for the marginalised cannot be separate from demand-side interventions to mitigate child labour (Chap. 6). In terms of malnutrition and anaemia, reducing the prevalence of sickness and school absenteeism and ensuring children begin primary school at the official age of six appear dependent upon reducing current levels of child stunting, malnutrition and especially anaemia, from which the majority of children suffer in the country (Chap. 5).

Other external variables seem to be less important than these five factors in influencing the educational landscape in Ghana. Regression analysis found parents without any schooling, particularly fathers, to be a predictor in constraining school participation, although interventions such as promoting adult literacy programmes may not always be the most viable policy response, since targeting children and youth directly would likely often have greater policy relevance and impact (Chap. 8). A rather unexpected finding from the regression results is the very limited or insignificant impact that the number of younger or older household members has on a child's schooling, whereas descriptive data analysis highlighted its importance on access and outcomes. Some issues have few effects on the education sector in Ghana compared to other sub-Saharan countries (e.g. HIV/AIDS, gender disparities in access at lower levels), and therefore should receive relatively lower levels of resources.

- How and to what extent does educational attainment influence political, economic, health and demographic factors in Ghana?

The analysis shows that—in a circular fashion—increasing levels of education has the potential, among other benefits, to relieve population pressure, help foster economic growth, generate high social and health returns and, possibly most importantly, improve people's quality of life.

Meeting other MDGs will be accelerated by greater educational attainment. While over one quarter of 15–19-year olds in the country and about half of Northerners of this age have not been able to achieve the modest goal of completing a full course of primary schooling by 2008/2009 (GDHS), various data analyses and regression findings in this study indicate that achieving universal primary education (MDG 2) and higher levels of education will help attain other MDGs, which continue to play a central role in the government's development strategy:

- **MDG 1 Eradicate extreme poverty and hunger**: Getting out-of-school children into the system and ensuring their progression throughout and possibly beyond the basic cycle will constitute a true hope for many to help escape poverty traps for themselves and their children later in life, as a Ghanaian's income level increases exponentially according to his or her educational status. Cost-benefit analysis also found high private and social rates of return to education in Ghana. It appears, therefore, that the 28.5 % of people in 2005/2006 living in poverty could be strongly reduced if all children and youth would in fact receive at least basic education (Chap. 6). In terms of hunger, the share of both chronically and severely undernourished/stunted children under-5 with mothers who have no schooling is about twice as high as for those with mothers who have upper secondary schooling or beyond (Chap. 5).
- **MDG 3 Promote gender equality and empower women**: Gender parity in access has nearly been reached at the basic school level, while there are two

males for every female at the tertiary level. Improving gender parity in educational attainment at all levels would help reduce gender inequalities in earnings, in types of employment and, amongst others, in holding public positions (Chaps. 6 and 7).

- **MDG 4 Reduce child mortality**: Children who have mothers without any schooling are more likely to die during infancy than those who have mothers who complete the basic school cycle (78 deaths compared to 52 deaths per 1,000 live births) (Multiple Indicator Cluster Survey 2006).
- **MDG 5 Improve maternal health**: Regression analysis indicates that a woman's progression up the educational ladder directly impacts her health and social behaviour in terms of childbearing, pregnancy, and natal care. Compared to women without any schooling, those with secondary education delay their first pregnancy by 2.7 years, space out pregnancies by an additional 6 and a half months, and seek more health care, with for example an 18 % increase in using a malaria prevention drug during pregnancy. It also found that if all girls would complete the basic cycle, they would have almost one less child later in life, whereas graduating from university explains a reduction of almost two childbirths per woman, while controlling for age, locality, occupation/wealth and physical access to a health facility (Chap. 5).
- **MDG 6 Combat HIV/AIDS, malaria and other diseases**: Only 1.6 % of men without schooling, who had two or more partners in the past year, used a condom in comparison to 18.2 % for those with primary education and 41.9 % of men who have at least upper secondary schooling, which is partly explained by sex education in schools providing students with knowledge and skills that can influence their behaviour and offer protection. Children who have mothers with upper secondary schooling or beyond are twice as likely to take anti-malarial drugs when they have fever (61.5 %) compared to those with mothers who have no schooling (31.7 %) (Chap. 5).
- **MDG 7 Ensure environmental sustainability**: While climate stress particularly affects Northern Ghana and continues to intensify in this part of the country (World Bank 2010d), the ability to mitigate it and other environmental hazards will be likely conditional on scaling up educational capital and technological efficiency in Ghana.

Improving education is a 'sine qua non' for a number of aspects of national development. Consolidating political participation, enhancing the quality of the country's labour force, making the economy more diversified and competitive, promoting sustainable social and economic development, sustainably fighting poverty and empowering individuals are central challenges confronting Ghanaians in years to come, as the data analysis has shown. Since tackling these challenges are all dependent on scaling up educational capital, it will be fundamental for the government to improve the delivery of educational services to effectively lay the needed skills and knowledge base.

Findings show that household occupation, health status, household demographics and economic welfare levels can help to predict a child's education opportunities early in life. The years of education he or she is able to acquire can help predict in turn their type of occupation, health status, household demographics and economic welfare levels later in life. In conditions of extreme education poverty, these interlocking synergies can at times reflect a 'catch 22' or education poverty trap, making public action absolutely necessary to tackle the numerous external constraints to school intake and retention. It is, therefore, argued here that education policy and strategy must not only be better aligned to the existing and emerging challenges identified in the analysis. But to provide more equitable opportunities and outcomes in education for all young Ghanaians, the education sector and a wider range of policy instruments cannot be separated from the overall external environment within which the sector operates and which presents constraints and opportunities that face the sector.

- In response to the key findings, what combinations of policies and programmes are likely to lead to the greatest access and attainment in Ghana especially for educationally deprived groups in years to come?

The true value of the analysis lies in the key findings and lessons derived from its data-driven diagnosis of the underlying factors influencing educational exclusion and progression and in its policy implications to better organise, rationalise and operate the education system. The fact that many of the current policy interventions appear either poorly fit or indifferent to a number of sectoral challenges identified in this analysis is a serious policy and institutional concern. In reducing the North–South educational gap, child labour and malnutrition, the policies and programmes that currently have the largest potential are either spatially blind (capitation grant), have a limited scope (LEAP), are very poorly—if not inversely—targeted ('deprived districts' scheme and school feeding programme) or suffer from a combination of these. This helps reflect the low capability of the government in administering well targeted, and relevant, efficient and effective policies and programmes, which has been identified here as possibly the most persistent binding constraint facing the education sector in Ghana. The sector has required an urgent review of prevailing interventions to realign policy with set targets and actual outcomes. The policy matrix mapped out in the preceding chapter addresses these various pressing issues and helps to facilitate policy prioritisation in a country with constrained resources and institutional capacity by outlining policy responses and reforms and their estimated costs and benefits. Based on this results- and capacity-focused roadmap, policy planners and makers could make informed, evidence-based decisions on possible ways to build up administrative and institutional capabilities, to enhance the efficiency of public expenditure and the effectiveness of public policies and programmes, and to increase access and outcomes at all levels by stimulating educational demand, and thereby achieve the second MDG and other education and development objectives in Ghana.

In terms of the most important external influences shaping the educational landscape in Ghana identified above, the policy matrix outlines strategic actions and reforms needed to tackle disparities between the North and South (e.g. redirect the capitation grant to the North), reduce malnutrition/anaemia (e.g. retarget the school feeding programme to the most needy) and minimise child labour (e.g. scale up LEAP in the North), while it only indirectly focuses on policy measures to help promote economic growth (e.g. set enrolment quotas to raise shares of science and technology students) and reduce population growth (e.g. increase levels of female education through distance-learning universities) (see Table 8.1 for an overview of policies and programmes to increase access and outcomes). A few of the proposed reforms and new interventions, although beyond the targeted scope of the study, will require comprehensive costing—a potential area for further research.

Coping Strategies

Overarching lessons learned and coping strategies for policy to improve the educational landscape are derived from the main findings:

1. *The education sector will have to better reflect external influences.* The regression results in Table 6.6 reveal that school context features (e.g. school distance) have a limited or insignificant impact on determining school attendance in Ghana, while background characteristics have much greater impact (e.g. residency in the North–South). A key finding of the analysis is that the effects of external factors (the primary focus of the study) on the inputs, disparities and outputs of the education sector by far outweigh the effects of school-specific factors (the primary focus of the government's resource allocations). About 96 % of total education expenditure is earmarked for teacher salaries, 3.6 % for administration and 0.4 % for service, while about 0.1 % for investment (EMIS 2010). A central implication is that education policy, programmes and resource allocations have to adjust to better reflect external circumstances at the individual, family, community and national level, on which decisions about educational access and completion are dependent. This will take two forms. First, education and skills development hinges on the successful design and implementation of interventions to reduce demographic growth, promote economic growth and facilitate the integration of the North with the rest of the country. Second, education policy, planning and service delivery will have to widen its instruments to better incorporate the specific needs of local communities (to which the current system is largely indifferent). Such a shift may require building up the capacity at the local level (in schools) to adapt to the key inhibitors of education in their specific communities.
2. *The Ministry of Education and other ministries need to recognise the intersectorality of these issues and execute programmes in closer collaboration with each other.* Universalising basic education will not be possible without strong reductions in child labour, and eliminating child labour will not be possible without nearing universal basic education. Universalising schooling in class one of primary appears to also rely on minimising

the incidence of malnutrition. Such interlocking relationships between non-participation in school, child labour and malnutrition require innovative policy approaches such as cash transfers to households conditional on no child labour involvement, health visits and attendance in school (possibly with a school feeding programme) in order to ensure that children complete at least the basic school cycle in Ghana. Of the external influences analysed here, the Government of Ghana (2003) has to date only recognised improved access to water and sanitation as a precondition to attain the second MDG (although over one-third of primary schools still have no access to drinking water and toilets). It is nonetheless hoped that this analysis may contribute to placing other priorities on the government's policy and programme agenda to reach universal education, above all malnutrition and child labour. It will furthermore be vital to better integrate and mainstream some of the various intersectoral issues discussed above into the departments, activities and programmes of the Ministry of Education, the Ministry of Health and other Ministries with education-related activities. For example, efforts aimed at combating child labour by the Ministry of Employment and Social Welfare, through its social protection strategy (World Bank and UNICEF 2009), will need to take its interdependencies with schooling into account in order to truly maximise success, for which greater inter-ministerial collaboration is required.

3. *A supply-driven policy is needed at initial expansion of each educational level but policy must become increasingly demand-driven as schooling universalises at each level.* The analysis found that education policy in Ghana that has been largely supply-driven (i.e. the government mainly just pays teachers and provides schools) has limited reach, effectiveness and sustainability in the process of improving equitable educational outcomes and has left out large shares of children and youth. A strong supply-driven strategy is necessary at initial expansion of a given level of education but as the share of the excluded becomes smaller, the need for demand-driven policies increases. Findings suggest that at a threshold of about 10–15 % of excluded children and youth supply-driven policies will likely achieve little, if anything at all. The time to shift towards demand-driven policies has come for the basic education level and may arrive in the coming years for the upper secondary level, so that further improvements will likely not be possible unless policy and institutional arrangements improve to better reflect the evolving reality in this new middle income country. Unless the objective and content of policy reforms begin targeting the remaining out-of-school children (located mainly in the highly agriculture-dependent North), better tackle their high opportunity costs for schooling and particularly better reflect the specific circumstances of child workers, it will remain very difficult, if not impossible, to attain fcuBE and other education targets at higher levels. Changing needs require, therefore, more coherent policy-planning and -sequencing to constantly maximise benefits.
4. *It is not always about mobilising the will of the government but rather building up its capability.* The Government of Ghana (relative to other West African countries) has pioneered two particularly innovative policy

approaches: the capitation grant and the LEAP programme (World Bank 2010e). The government's adoption of these two policies, together with the sector receiving one-third of total public spending and the government's policy of free basic education, provides evidence of its strong support for the education sector. However, the analysis shows that the capitation grant and the LEAP programme, and a number of other policy instruments often are poorly monitored, ineffectively implemented, leak resources and fall short of meeting set objectives and outcomes (Chap. 8). This fact, coupled with the strong geographic distribution and expansion of private schools in rural areas (which are typically poor areas), implies that the government may often be willing but not always capable to drive educational development. To tackle the key binding constraint of low capacity in the government, policy solutions are outlined in Table 8.1 that would help build up administrative and institutional capabilities and thereby raise the efficiency and effectiveness of policy instruments and strengthen organisational arrangements. The implication is that the question of whether the available resource pool can be utilised in a different, better targeted and more efficient way to reach the underserved and attain better outcomes is generally just as important as asking if the government is allocating sufficient resources.

Emerging Challenges and Opportunities

Several challenges and opportunities emerge from the analysis and can be grouped into the following areas:

- *How to best accommodate for the needs of a smaller out-of-school population that is even more disadvantaged than in past years*? With the national share having reduced from about one in four to one in six 6–14 year olds out of school between 1993/1994 and 2008/2009, it is possible—although much more difficult—to continue making gains attracting the last 15 % of excluded children into the system if policy levers and reforms such as those outlined in Chap. 8 are effectively implemented. It is worth stressing that the education sector experienced phases of expansion in the past but gains have not always been successfully consolidated, reiterating the vital importance of scaling up the system's capacity and of continual policy analysis and planning to maximise policy impact. The final push towards universal basic schooling will not be attained rapidly, as the last 5–10 % are extremely marginalised and likely to account for the largest share of undernourished/anaemic child labourers who live in isolated, agricultural communities of the North. As the group of the most educationally marginalised becomes smaller and much more difficult to reach, the number of multiple interlocking risk factors increases and the specific background traits (and therefore policy priorities) change (see e.g. Fig. 7.3). Likewise, ensuring progression beyond the initial classes of primary and even

the primary cycle for these children will be accompanied by another set of difficult challenges that will also demand targeted and innovative policy responses.
- *How to build consensus with differing individual and social needs, and public and private interests*? In discussing policy responses, planners and practitioners will need to balance different (sometimes conflicting) demands at the same time: achieving desirable national outcomes, fulfilling the educational needs and ambitions of every child and youth, meeting the private sector's specific demands for skilled labour and attaining outcomes which are viable both financially and within a given time period. Establishing a coalition or network to bring various stakeholders together could help build consensus around these issues.
- *Should the expenditure structure be revised to mobilise more resources for higher levels of education (promoting skills development) or for lower levels (promoting fcuBE)*? Regression analysis has provided evidence that increasing the national share of primary graduates can be a vital policy tool to improve health and social outcomes (Chap. 5) and reduce demographic growth in the country (Chap. 7). Increasing levels of education in secondary and beyond would not only promote these benefits, but also drive the country's skills development and diversification (Chap. 3) and multiply people's levels of income and the private and social rates of return as cost-benefit analysis shows (Chap. 6). The question of whether to continue allocating the high budgetary shares to the primary sub-sector at almost half of all education expenditure (2008 EMIS data) as in many low-income sub-Saharan countries or begin incrementally redistributing these shares towards higher levels of education to help tackle the skills gap and to better reflect the expenditure structure in more developed countries will need to be discussed by policy planners especially for a country recently transitioning into the group of middle-income countries. To consolidate this transition, the country will require a better educated and better skilled labour force to improve the planning, delivery and management in basic social services like education and in infrastructure and other sectors. It is argued here that gradually shifting the budgetary shares to higher levels of education may be a viable approach given that a number of policy and reform approaches to enhance the efficiency of public spending proposed in the preceding chapter would, if adopted effectively, help achieve basic education for all with likely lower than current levels of public expenditure.

The present study has attempted to help address these emerging challenges, while they are areas that may demand further research. The emerging challenges combined with the current obstacles to accessing and completing different levels of education are pressing, the individual and societal damages accrued from the educationally underserved and excluded are irreversible and the effects of factors outside the classroom on educational development are significant, so that the national objective of raising Ghanaians' education and skills base must be addressed differently and much more aggressively.

In spite of the numerous challenges identified and outlined in the analysis, there is optimism about the country's educational development. It is arguable that efforts towards closing in on the target of universal basic completion have been a catalyst in advancing social and economic conditions in the country, perhaps, more than any other policy. The current generation of Ghanaians has within its reach the opportunity of being the first generation to reach the underserved (largely through better targeted programme mechanisms) and ensure that every child has access to and completes at least 9 years of education. This aspiration is dependent on a sound, data-driven understanding of the underlying causes of educational deprivation and, based on this understanding, outlining a comprehensive package of needed reforms. These are the central contributions at the core of this analysis: first, identifying which external constraints and enabling factors are most important and, second, which policy and reform approaches are best in promoting the educational status of Ghanaian children and youth. Each step is incomplete without the other; combined they are critical for planners and policy makers to improve the educational landscape in Ghana.

Possibly the most important lessons learned here are that attaining the second MDG, fcuBE and other national education objectives such as a more skilled labour force will be undermined even in the medium or long term, unless (1) continual monitoring of educational needs and outcomes and the causes of educational deprivation via data analysis (needed for sound evidence-based planning) is conducted, (2) respective policy responses and reform packages that are solid and coherent and disproportionately target the most disadvantaged are outlined and effectively implemented, and (3) policy instruments and institutional arrangements are continually assessed, fine-tuned and reformed to maximise their targeting, relevance, efficiency and effectiveness, and thereby to ensure the public resource pool is used most efficiently and has the largest possible impact. This analysis attempts to make a contribution towards helping to achieve these preconditions and these education objectives. It is worth reiterating that these education objectives are only achievable if the most marginalised children and youth, who are geographically isolated, have poor nutritional status and/or are working, are positively discriminated so that they can benefit from at least a complete cycle of basic education. Because these objectives are the cornerstone of the government's national development strategy, and because the steps needed to achieve them have been outlined, the government needs to now deliver on its commitment.

References

Afrobarometer. 2008. *Data of Round 4 Afrobarometer Survey in Ghana*. Afrobarometer together with Center for Democracy and Development, www.afrobarometer.org, (data downloaded on 4 May 2011).

Akyeampong, Kwame. 2004. *Aid for Self-Help Effort?: A sustainable alternative route to Basic Education in Northern Ghana*. Brighton: University of Sussex, Centre for International Education.

Akyeampong, Kwame; Jerome Djamgmah; Abena Oduro; Alhassan Seidu; and Frances Hunt. 2007. *Access to Basic Education in Ghana: The Evidence and Issues*. Sussex: CREATE, Country Analytical Report.

AllAfrica/IRIN. 2007. Child Labour Photo. Nairobi: UN Office for the Coordination of Humanitarian Affairs; Photo taken by: Manoocher Deghati

Awedoba, Albert; P. Stanley Yoder; Kristi Fair; and Stephanie Gorin. 2003. *Household demand for schooling in Ghana*. Maryland USA: ISSER/USAID.

Boafo-Arthur, Kwame. 2008. *Democracy and Stability in West Africa: The Ghanaian Experience*. Uppsala: Uppsala University, Department of Peace and Conflict Research, Claude Ake Memorial Papers No. 4.

Boateng, Kwabia; and Edward Ofori-Sarpong. 2002. *An Analytical Study of the Labour Market for Tertiary Graduates in Ghana*. Accra: World Bank/National Council for Tertiary Education and National Accreditation Board Project Report.

Buchmann, Claudia; and Emily Hannum. 2001. *Education and Stratification in Developing Countries: A Review of Theories and Research*. In: Annual Review of Sociology, Vol. 27, pp. 77–102.

Canagarajah, Sudharshan; and Harold Coulombe. 1997. *Child Labor and Schooling in Ghana*. Washington DC: World Bank, Economic and Sector Work.

CDD. 2010. Draft version: *Public Expenditure Tracking Survey: Tracking Capitation Grant In Primary Schools in Ghana*. Accra: Center for Democratic Development (CDD).

Chandra, Vandana; and Israel Osorio-Rodarte. 2007. *Options for Export Diversification and Faster Export Growth in Ghana*. Washington DC: The World Bank.

De La Cruz, Natalie; Benjamin Crookston; Kirk Dearden; Bobbi Gray; Natasha Ivins; Stephen Alder; and Robb Davis. 2006. *Who sleeps under bednets in Ghana? A doer/non-doer analysis of malaria prevention behaviours*. In: Malaria Journal, Vol. 5, No. 61.

Dzator, Janet; and John Asafu-Adjaye. 2004. *A study of malaria care provider choice in Ghana*. In: Health Policy, Vol. 69, No. 3, pp. 389–401.

EARC. 2003. *Teacher Time on Task*. United States Agency for International Development, unpublished report. Accra: Educational Assessment and Research Center.

A. Krauss, *External Influences and the Educational Landscape*, SpringerBriefs in Economics, DOI: 10.1007/978-1-4614-4936-2,

Education Management Information System (EMIS). 2011. *Education Management Information System (EMIS) Data*. Accra: Ministry of Education, for this analysis both raw and clean EMIS data-files are used that have been provided by the government and cover all years of data collected.

Fentiman, Alicia; Andrew Hall; and Donald Bundy. 1999. *School Enrolment Patterns in Rural Ghana: a comparative study of the impact of location, gender, age and health on children's access to basic schooling*. In: Comparative Education, Vol. 35, No. 3, pp. 331–349.

Fentiman, Alicia; Andrew Hall; and Don Bundy. 2001. *Health and cultural factors associated with enrollment in basic education: a study in rural Ghana*. In: Social Science and Medicine, Vol. 52, pp. 429–439.

Fobil, Julius; and Ireneous Soyiri. 2006. *An assessment of government policy response to HIV/AIDS in Ghana*. In: Journal of Social Aspects of HIV/AIDS, Vol. 3 No. 2, pp. 457–465.

Freedom House. 2010. *Map of Freedom in the World*. http://www.freedomhouse.org/template.cfm?page=363&year=2010, (accessed 20 September 2011).

Ghana Demographic and Health Survey (GDHS). 2009 and 1994. *Ghana Demographic and Health Survey*. Accra: Ghana Statistical Service; cleaned data set; available through http://www.measuredhs.com.

Ghana Health Service. 2010. *National HIV Prevalence and AIDS Estimates Report 2009–2015*. Accra: Ghana Health Service, Ministry of Health.

Ghana Living Standards Survey (GLSS). 2006. *Ghana Living Standards Survey*. Accra: Ghana Statistical Service; cleaned data set.

Ghana Living Standards Survey (GLSS). 2008. *Ghana Living Standards Survey: Report of the Fifth Round*. Accra: Ghana Statistical Service.

Ghana National Commission on Children (GNCC). 2000. *Ghana's children: the child's perspective*. Accra: GNCC.

Ghana Statistical Service (GSS). 2003. *Core Welfare Indicators Questionnaire*. Accra: Ghana Statistical Service.

Ghana Statistical Service (GSS). 2010. *Information Paper on Economic Statistics: Rebasing of Ghana's National Accounts to Reference Year 2006*. Accra: Ghana Statistical Service, published November, http://www.mofep.gov.gh/documents/RebasingNationalAccountsGhana.pdf.

Ghanaweb. 2011. *Foreign Exchange Rates*. Accra: Government of Ghana, http://www.ghanaweb.com/GhanaHomePage/economy/forex.php, (accessed 11 July 2011).

Glewwe, Paul; and Hanan Jacoby. 1994. *Student Achievement and Schooling Choice in Low-Income Countries: Evidence from Ghana*. Wisconsin: University of Wisconsin Press, in: The Journal of Human Resources, Vol. 29, No. 3, pp. 843–864.

Glewwe, Paul; and Nauman Ilias. 1996. *The determinants of school attainment in sub-Saharan Africa: A case study of Ghana*. Washington DC: World Bank, Policy Research Department, in: Journal of International Development, Vol. 8, No. 3, pp. 395–413.

Government of Ghana. 1992. *The Constitution of the Republic of Ghana*. Accra: Government of Ghana.

Government of Ghana. 2003. *Education Strategic Plan 2003 to 2015*. Accra: Ministry of Education, Vol. 1, May.

Government of Ghana. 2006. *Ghanadistricts*. A Public-Private Partnership Programme between Ministry of Local Government and Rural Development and Maks Publications & Media Services,http://www.ghanadistricts.com/districts1on1/asuogyaman/?arrow=atd&_=67&sa=1860, (last accessed 15 September 2011).

Government of Ghana. 2009. *Ghana School Feeding Programme: Annual Operating Plan 2009*. Accra: Government of Ghana.

Govindasamy, Ramu *et al.* 2006. *Impediments to Marketing African Natural products from Ghana: Preliminary Results*. Paper Prepared for Presentation at the American Agricultural Economics Association Annual Meeting, Long Beach, California, July 23–26.

Gylfason, Thorvaldur; and Gylfi Zoega. 2003. *Education, social equality and economic growth: A view of the landscape*. CESifo: Working Paper no. 876, Category 5.

Haynes, Jeff. 1993. *Sustainable Democracy in Ghana? Problems and Prospects*. In: Third World Quarterly, Vol. 14, No. 3, Democratisation in the Third World, pp. 451–467.

International Labour Organisation (ILO). 2008. *Child labour statistics: 18th International Conference of Labour Statisticians*. Geneva: ILO, ICLS/18/2008/III.

International Monetary Fund (IMF). 2009. *Ghana: 2009 Article IV Consultation*. Washington DC: IMF.

Jolliffe, Dean. 2002. *Whose Education Matters in the Determination of Household Income? Evidence from a Developing Country*. The University of Chicago Press: Economic Development and Cultural Change, Vol. 50, No. 2, pp. 287–312.

Joseph, George; and Sonia Plaza. 2010. *Remittances and Child Labor in Ghana*. Unpublished powerpoint presentation for: the IZA Workshop on The Africa Migration Project, in collaboration with the World Bank, presented on 4 June 2011.

Krauss, Alexander. 2011. *Skills Development in Cambodia: The supply of education and skills, employment dynamics and the demand of the labour market*. World Bank, Social Protection Department, unpublished technical background paper.

Kwapong, Olivia. 2007. *Widening access to tertiary education for women in Ghana through distance education*. In: Turkish Online Journal of Distance Education-TOJDE, Vol. 8, No.4, Art. 5.

Little, Angela. 2010. *Access to Basic Education in Ghana: politics, policies and progress*. Sussex: University of Sussex, and CREATE, Research Monograph No. 42, August.

MARA (Mapping Malaria Risk in Africa). 2004. *Mapping Malaria Risk in Africa*. Durban, South Africa: MARA, available through http://www.mara.org.za/.

Ministry of Education. 2008. *Preliminary Education Sector Performance Report*. Accra: MOESS.

Ministry of Education. 2009. *Education Strategic Plan 2010 to 2020*. Accra: Government of Ghana, September.

Ministry of Education. 2010. *Draft Education Sector Performance Report*. Accra: Ministry of Education, unpublished version for internal circulation and development partner discussion.

Ministry of Local Government and Rural Development. 2006. *Ghana Districts*. Accra: Government of Ghana, http://www.ghanadistricts.com.

Moss, Todd; and Lauren Young. 2009. *Saving Ghana from Its Oil: The Case for Direct Cash Distribution*. CGD Working Paper 186. Washington DC: Center for Global Development.

Multiple Indicator Cluster Survey. 2006. *Monitoring the situation of children, women, and men*. Accra: Ghana Statistical Service.

NDPC (National Development Planning Commission). 2005. *Growth and Poverty Reduction Strategy (GPRS II)*. Accra: Government of Ghana, 2006–2009.

Netherlands Development Organisation. 2008. *One meal, many benefits? A National Inventory of the Ghana School Feeding Programme*. Accra: SNV Ghana.

Nketiah-Amponsah, Edward. 2009. *Public spending and economic growth: evidence from Ghana (1970-2004)*. In: Development Southern Africa, Vol. 26, No. 3, pp. 477–497.

Nsowah-Nuamah, Nicholas; Francis Teal; and Moses Awoonor-Williams. 2010. *Jobs, Skills and Incomes in Ghana: How was poverty halved?* In collaboration with DfID, the ESRC and the IDRC.

Oseil, Robert; and Peter Quartey. 2001. *The HIPC Initiative and Poverty Reduction in Ghana: An Assessment*. United Nations University, Discussion Paper No. 2001/119.

Pritchett, Lant. 2004. *Access to Education*, in: Global Crises, Global Solutions. Bjorn Lomborg. Cambridge: Cambridge University Press, pp. 175–234.

Ray, Debraj. 1998. *Economia del desarrollo*. Barcelona: Antoni Bosch, originally by Princeton University Press.

Rolleston, Caine; and Moses Oketch. 2007. *Educational expansion in Ghana: Economic assumptions and expectations*. In: International Journal of Educational Development, Vol. 28, pp. 320–339.

Teal, Francis. 2001. *Education, incomes, poverty and inequality in Ghana in the 1990s*. Oxford: Oxford University, Centre for the Study of African Economies, Working paper WPS/2001.21., paper 159.

The Economist. 2010. *Mining in Ghana - Carats and sticks: A resource-rich government takes on foreign mining firms*. The Economist print edition, Mar 31 2010.

UNAIDS. 2010. *Country Situation: Ghana*. Accra: UNAIDS http://data.unaids.org/pub/FactSheet/2008/sa08_gha_en.pdf, (accessed 19 September 2011).

UNESCO. 2010. *EFA Global Monitoring Report; Reaching the Marginalized.* Paris: UNESCO; and, Oxford: Oxford University Press.

UN Population data. 2010. *World Population Prospects: The 2008 Revision.* Population Division of the Department of Economic and Social Affairs of the United Nations Secretariat, http://esa.un.org/unpp, (accessed 26 April 2010).

Van Evera, Stephen. 1997. *Guide to methods for students of political science.* Ithaca, New York: Cornell University Press.

Vuri, D. 2008. *The effect of availability and distance to school on children's time allocation in Ghana and Guatemala.* Rome: University of Rome, Understanding Children's Work (UCW) Project, Working Paper.

WHO. 2010. *Guidelines for the treatment of malaria, second edition.* Geneva: WHO.

World Bank. 2002. *Opening Doors; Education and the World Bank.* Washington DC: World Bank.

World Bank. 2003. *School Education in Nigeria: Preparing for Universal Basic Education.* Washington DC: World Bank, Human Development - Africa Region.

World Bank. 2004. *Cost, Financing and School Effectiveness of Education in Malawi: A future of limited choices and endless opportunities.* Washington DC: World Bank, Development Research Group.

World Bank. 2004a. *Books, Buildings and Learning Outcomes: An impact evaluation of World Bank support to basic education in Ghana.* Washington, DC: World Bank.

World Bank. 2009. *Atlas of Global Development: second edition.* Washington DC: World Bank by Collins Geo.

World Bank. 2009a. *Job Creation and Skills Development.* Washington DC: World Bank, Report No. 40328-GH.

World Bank. 2009b. *Ghana: Economy-Wide Impact of Oil Discovery in Ghana.* Washington DC: World Bank, PREM 4, Africa Region, Report No. 47321-GH.

World Bank. 2009c. *The Capacity Development Results Framework: A strategic and results-oriented approach to learning for capacity development.* Washington DC: World Bank, authors: Samuel Otoo, Natalia Agapitova and Joy Behrens.

World Bank. 2010. *The Education System in Malawi.* Washington DC: World Bank, Working Paper No. 182.

World Bank. 2010a. *Outlook for Remittance Flows 2011–12: Recovery after the crisis, but risks lie ahead,* in: Migration and Development Brief 13. Washington DC: World Bank.

World Bank. 2010b. *Country Assistance Strategy Progress Report for the Republic of Ghana.* Washington DC: World Bank, West Africa Country Department, Report No. 52988-GH.

World Bank. 2010c. *The Education System in Swaziland: Training and Skills Development for Shared Growth and Competitiveness.* Washington DC: World Bank, Africa Region Human Development Department, principal author Mmantsetsa Marope.

World Bank. 2010d. *Tackling Poverty from Northern Ghana.* Washington DC: World Bank, PREM 4, May 31.

World Bank. 2010e. *Improving the targeting of social programs in Ghana.* Washington DC: World Bank, Development Dialogue on Values and Ethics; Draft for Internal Discussion, June 30, 2010.

World Bank. 2011. *Education in Ghana: Improving Equity, Efficiency and Accountability of Education Service Delivery.* Washington DC: World Bank, principal authors: Peter Darvas and Alexander Krauss.

World Bank and UNICEF. 2009. *Abolishing School Fees in Africa: Lessons from Ethiopia, Ghana, Kenya, Malawi, and Mozambique.* Washington DC: World Bank in collaboration with UNICEF.

World Development Indicators Database. 2011. *World Development Indicators; EdStats Database; Africa Development Indicators.* http://data.worldbank.org/data-catalog, (last accessed 19 September 2011).

Biography

Alexander Krauss holds a Ph.D. in Development Economics. He has spent the last 6 years analysing issues related to human development, labour markets, social safety nets and poverty. The past five years have involved working mainly with the World Bank, primarily in the Ghana and Liberia country offices, and with the Inter-American Development Bank in the Colombia country office. His recent work has been advising the Government of Liberia on its national planning process. He has also analysed policy issues related to skills, training and labour opportunities and outcomes in the Republic of the Congo and Cambodia. His other research interests are in connecting policy with subjective well-being (life satisfaction) and environmental sustainability.

A. Krauss, *External Influences and the Educational Landscape*,
SpringerBriefs in Economics, DOI: 10.1007/978-1-4614-4936-2,

MIX
Papier aus verantwortungsvollen Quellen
Paper from responsible sources
FSC® C105338

If you have any concerns about our products,
you can contact us on
ProductSafety@springernature.com

In case Publisher is established outside the EU,
the EU authorized representative is:
Springer Nature Customer Service Center GmbH
Europaplatz 3, 69115 Heidelberg, Germany

Printed by Libri Plureos GmbH
in Hamburg, Germany